THE WINNING OF AFRICA

The Life and Times of Eliudi Issangya

Daniel Simmering

The Winning of Africa:
The Life and Times of Eliudi Issangya

Udpated Edition 2023

By Daniel Simmering

Layout by Bill Asher

Copyright © 2023, Daniel Simmering

ISBN: 978-1-942661-01-6

All rights reserved. No part of this book may be reproduced or transmitted in any form or by any means, electronic or mechanical, including photocopying, recording or by any information storage and retrieval system, without written permission from the author, except for the inclusion of brief quotations in a review.

Published by Kitsap Publishing
www.KitsapPublishing.com

Dedication

This book is dedicated first and foremost to God. Without His inspiration and guidance, this book would not have been written. Second, I dedicate this book to Gene and Lorraine Anderson whose unwavering support and encouragement during the writing of this book was a tremendous blessing. Lastly, I dedicate this book to my wife, Gloria, who juggled our family schedule and finances which allowed me to complete the book.

Special Thank You

I truly want thank all of the people who donated their stories to me so that I could include them in this book. It was a joy for me to hear each one of those personal recollections. Without those stories, there would not be a biography of Eliudi Issangya. I also want to thank all of those people who spent hours proof-reading and doing other time consuming tasks that improved this story of Eliudi's life. To all of you, a huge thank you.

Special Note

It is intended that all net proceeds from this book will be donated to support Bishop Eliudi's operations in Tanzania and other parts of Africa.

INTRODUCTION

How is anyone able to predict who the Lord will use in ways that are beyond the norm? Scripture reveals that God chooses the humble rather than the proud; the poor, even the foolish, of this world to confound the wise.

No one could have foreseen that an ordinary, poor, African dirt farmer would be chosen to have such a large impact on the lives of countless thousands of unsaved Africans.

But that is the story of Bishop Eliudi Issangya, a common farmer in Tanzania who looked up in the sky one day and declared that he would fly on huge transcontinental jets. As a consequence of the fulfillment of that vow, he changed the lives of so many of his own people as well as those in far destinations.

This story reflects the power of God to call the humble and the willing to do remarkable things. This is the story of an answered call by a man who believed God, who has witnessed miracles, and remains committed to a life of evangelism.

Garven and Judy Kinley

International Evangelism Outreach

This map of Tanzania is meant to show the reader the location of the village of Sakila. It is not intended to show all the geographic features or cities in Tanzania. Sakila's name on the map is in bold and large letters to make it easier for the viewer of the map to find. Indeed, it is a small village in the foot hills of Mt. Kilimanjaro.

PART 1:
Casting The Vision

CHAPTER 1:

I KNOW THAT MY REDEEMER LIVES

(Job 19:25)

In 2008 an evangelical team consisting of about 35 high school-aged students from Texas was visiting the International Evangelism Centre campus in Sakila, Tanzania. In conjunction with the African students who were studying at the School of Evangelism, the Americans were conducting revival meetings for the local people. During the team's visitation, a trip to an outlying village was also scheduled. That village was about 70 kilometers away from Sakila and located near the base of Mt. Kilimanjaro. The plan was for Bishop Eliudi and his driver to journey in a truck to the village to transport all the supplies and materials required to conduct the crusade. They would reach the village and start assembling equipment for the high school students who would arrive about 30 minutes later. Since an overnight stay was planned, a large amount of support equipment was essential. Behind the supply truck would be the bus carrying the high school girls, with the boys' bus following along last.

On a very dry and hot morning, the caravan started out to visit the remote village. The dirt roads to that village were narrow and rutted, resulting in an unpleasant, bumpy ride for the gospel team. Volcanic ash rolled in through the open windows whenever one of the buses slowed down. The bus riders' hair and clothing were being coated with the reddish-white dust as it billowed in the windows and settled on each of them.

At times tree branches and brush would scrape both sides of the busses as they struggled over the steep, narrow one-lane dirt road to the African village. The busses frequently had to dodge around donkeys whose primary job was carrying large plastic containers brimming with potable water. Trying to stay out of the deep ruts in the road, motorcycles occasionally came directly at the busses causing the bus driver to madly jerk the steering wheel to keep from hitting the motorcycles. To make matters worse, the Tanzanian road crews had installed large speed bumps every so often to prevent the motorcycles from traveling too fast. Those speed bumps would launch the busses into the air if they were driven over at any speed faster than a crawl.

During the trip to the village the bus carrying the girls stopped for a bathroom break. That stop forced the boys' bus to take the lead from the girls' bus as the journey continued through the African countryside.

As the lead truck, which was loaded with supplies, bounced along the road, the driver noticed in the distance that two individuals were standing in the middle of the dusty road. As they drove closer, Eliudi observed that the two men had revolvers in their possession and that their weapons were being held in a threatening manner. Another man was leaning on a tree along the left side of the road near some motorcycles with a fourth individual standing on the right side of the road, pointing his weapon at the cab of the truck. Eliudi and the truck driver knew that they could be in serious trouble. They were well aware of what the men's intentions were. The supply truck's driver slowly drew up to the bandits and reluctantly stopped on the dirt road.

Brandishing their weapons, the robbers demanded the truck's occupants turn over a half million shillings to them immediately. (In 2008, that amount of money was worth about $350 in US currency.) Eliudi coolly and with a steady voice told the men to relax as he had the money that they stipulated and he would give it to them. However, after he gave them the amount requested, the bandits wanted more and seized Eliudi's and his driver's wallets and their cell phones.

During the robbery, one of the bandits quizzed Eliudi about what he did for a living. When Eliudi was giving the robber his wallet and phone, he said he was a Tanzanian Bishop. Eliudi also nervously warned, "You fellows should not be doing this. We are men on a mission for the Lord and you are stealing from God when you rob us." Because governmental Bishops possess a lot of respect in Tanzania, the robbers became concerned and started to back off their aggressive stance. They were aware that they were not robbing just any truck driver and his passenger. Rapidly the bandits jumped on their motorcycles with their loot and roared off down the road in the direction from which Eliudi had come.

After saying a short prayer of thanksgiving for God's protection, Bishop Eliudi got on the CB radio and called the home base in Sakila to report what had happened.

The next vehicle that the bandits encountered on the dusty road was the bus carrying the young men from Texas. The robbers stopped and boarded the bus while brandishing their weapons and demanding money from the boys on the bus. The kids from Texas complied by giving up one and five US dollar bills to the crooks. The robbers were confused by the American money, not knowing if they were amassing a lot of cash or not. When they demanded more money, the students threw in ten dollar bills. The bewildered robbers soon realized that they were running out of time to make their get-away. When the quartet had collected what they could in the shortest amount of time, the bandits fled the bus, put away their guns, jumped on their motorcycles and sped away in a cloud of dust.

While the motorcycles were disappearing in the distance, the girls' bus rolled onto the scene. The robbers were in such a hurry to flee the scene of the crime that they did not even attempt to steal from the second bus and as a result girls were not robbed.

As the day's events unfolded, Bishop Eliudi knew that God had been their protection. The situation could have ended a lot worse than it did. As it was, no one had been hurt in the armed robbery. The bandits had only gotten away with some identification cards, cell phones and money. What the Bishop was most worried about was the real danger that the high school students had encountered. Eliudi was deeply regretful that this incident had happened. He was also concerned about what would happen when volunteers who were thinking of coming to Sakila heard of this incident.

As a result of the CB call that Bishop Eliudi had placed to his home campus, the school staff immediately notified the Tanzanian authorities of the robbery incident. The report of the theft went up the chain of command with even the Prime Minister of Tanzania being notified of the event. (Foreigners spend a lot of money in Tanzania and are treated with the utmost care.) Within an hour, a military detachment was ordered out along with a police SWAT team to locate and arrest the bandits. The authorities quickly arrived near the base of Mt. Kilimanjaro to begin searching for the culprits. An intense pursuit was conducted using all available manpower and equipment. Within a matter of three hours, one bandit was apprehended. After the first person was arrested and had confessed, he disclosed the identities of the other robbers and where they could be found. Before dawn of the next day, all of the remaining wanted fugitives were in police custody.

An investigation revealed that the bandits were members of a local gang. The police were able to retrieve most of the stolen goods and return it to their rightful owners. The four bandits, on the other hand, were convicted in short order and sent to jail. All four men would be dead within two years from suicide or diseases contacted in their African prison.

For Bishop Eliudi Issangya, operating an international evangelistic endeavor had never been totally easy. There was always something developing that needed his attention. Bandits on a lonely, isolated road at the base of Africa's highest mountain were just one of his problems. However, the robbery had been a particularly stressful problem. But like his other difficulties, God would guide Eliudi through each new day, all of which would have its own challenges to contend with. For a man who started out as a poor dirt farmer in Africa, he had risen to a position where he was leading an international church that had many mission-related aspects. By relying on God, Eliudi has accomplished what most people would consider to be humanly impossible.

Until recent times, vast portions of the African continent were thought of by Westerners as some of the most mysterious and exotic places on this planet. The coastline of Africa was well known to the crews of early European and American sailing ships. However, just a few miles from the shore, the unexplored interior of Africa received the dubious reputation of being the "dark continent." In the years preceding 1800 much of those undocumented areas on the maps of Africa were left blank and marked "terra incognita." Except for a few navigable rivers into the interior of the continent, no Western mapmaker had ever been to those "empty" places to survey the topography. The cartographers of the time had no geographical data of any sort to sketch onto those troubling and beckoning voids.

Western explorers came to Africa to journey into those undocumented lands in order to fill in the blank spots. The quest for acquiring knowledge, spreading religion and establishing trade were the driving forces for many of the expeditions that started in the area now known as Tanzania. Those pursuits continued from there to cross the breadth of Central Africa. European explorers, such as Richard Burton and John Speke, walked from the Indian Ocean coast into the interior to try to discover the source of the Nile River in 1857. Later, David Livingstone would suffer failing health and financially isolate himself in the interior of Africa while preaching the gospel of Jesus Christ to the native population. A newspaper reporter by the name of Henry Stanley would spend death-defying months in 1871 searching for Dr. Livingstone. Stanley would find Livingstone living in poverty on the shores of Lake Tanganyika in the western portion of what is today's Tanzania.

Most of those Western explorers who survived their journeys later went home to author best-selling books about their harrowing adventures in Africa. They also freely shared what map making information they had discovered. The majority of that knowledge was acquired at a dreadful price to all involved. In their popular books and news articles of the time, the explorers also pleaded with the reading public to take immediate humanitarian action to assist the native people of Africa who were being decimated by slave trading.

In the European rush to colonize Africa, an area that included Tanzania came under German rule in 1885 through trickery and a show of military might. This colony became known as German East Africa. The colonization of Africa exacted a price from the native land and its indigenous people. Natural resources were taken from the colonial territory, shipped to the occupying European country for their use or sold elsewhere to the highest bidder. The sisal plant was introduced in 1892 from Mexico to the farmers of German East Africa. (This plant is used to make twine and is still grown to this day in Tanzania for export.) During the decades after 1890, native farmers begrudgingly grew crops such as cotton, which they were forced to cultivate to meet the demands of the German government.

Even though Africa was being exploited, a number of colonial administrations did bestow some benefits on the native people. The slave trade, which was devastating the native population, was severely curtailed by most of the foreign governments. Wars between resident tribes were suppressed, forcing the people to live in a semi-peaceful coexistence.

(And who could forget that the movie, "The African Queen," was set in German East Africa?)

The German government encouraged its citizens to settle and homestead in its east African colony. In 1906 the Von Trappe family from Germany acquired a tract of land to farm on the southern slopes of Mt. Meru, which is in present-day northeastern Tanzania. To graze their cattle, they used large areas of the current Arusha National Park as a range for their livestock. (Some of the Von Trappe family descendants were the Von Trappes of the World War II-era who would become famous as a result of the movie "The Sound of Music.") When the Von Trappe family moved from Mt. Meru, they voluntarily set aside a large portion of their estate as a game sanctuary. That range land became part of Ngurdoto Crater National Park in 1960. When Mt. Meru was absorbed into the park in 1967, the name was changed to Arusha National Park.

After World War I, the League of Nations removed control of the east African colony from Germany and gave it to the British to administer. Even though conditions were still primitive, the human population of the area that would become Tanzania prospered and grew.

In the vast expanse of land near Mt. Kilimanjaro, the farming tribe known as Meru was also growing. One extended family of three brothers decided to move from their crowded village to a new area to homestead a farm. They packed up their belongings and traveled twenty-five kilometers to a place called Sakila. This new location was situated around 4,100 feet in elevation and in a lush valley between Mt. Meru and Mt. Kilimanjaro. Since the area was sparsely populated, that nearly virgin land was theirs for occupying it. The three brothers laid claim to about 250 acres of fertile farm land nestled between imposing mountainous and forested ridges.

At the time when the three brothers moved to their homestead, wild animals roamed freely over the territory. Once the family group had settled in and crops were growing, constant vigils were maintained to keep the wild animals away from their fields. At night, watchmen would light bonfires and walk around the farms with lit torches to ward off lions, hippopotamuses and other beasts. Impalas, giraffes and African buffalos could be simply driven away from the fields by screaming threats and the throwing of sticks or rocks. What worked well to ward off elephants was to come at the beasts with a flaming torch and the ringing of bells. These constant struggles saved the family's food supply and their livelihood.

The real trouble came when a wild animal became accustomed to the abundant and easily obtained food at the farm and could not be scared away. Of those animals, rhinoceros were particularly troublesome pests. With their poor eye sight, they could not be warded off without difficulty and would return repeatedly to raid the fields.

At that time, the Meru family at Sakila did not have guns to protect themselves or their crops. With wooden spears as their major means of defense, a troublesome rhinoceros could only be deterred by killing it. The practiced procedure of eradicating a rhinoceros put the farmers in grave danger. Two men with spears in hand would stand beside each other and verbally challenge the rhinoceros to charge them. They knew that a short tempered rhinoceros would only take so much ridicule before it would attack. As the rhinoceros rushed at the men, they would stand with spears ready and muscles tensed. At the last second, the brave farmers would quickly step in opposite directions at right angles to the rhinoceros' line of attack. The men would then turn toward the rhinoceros, rapidly lower their spears and try to impale the rhinoceros in the rib cage as it raced by. While doing this they had to keep in mind that they had to avoid the punishing rhino horns and head butts. The farmers knew that to come in contact with the horns of a charging rhino meant being crippled for life, but only if they succeeded in escaping death. If the farmers were lucky, the spears hit a vital organ and the rhinoceros would die before it returned for another attack.

However, the one creature which the brothers feared most was the white colonialist. The native family could fend off wild beasts, but when the Europeans wanted the native's land they took it. The brothers were always concerned that the colonial homesteaders would see their fertile valley and simply confiscate it from them. Luckily for the Meru family in Sakila, their farms were a distance off of the well-traveled roads between Moshi and Arusha.

One of the three brothers who settled in Sakila was named Ndelekwa Selembo Issangya. Since plural marriages were common among the Meru, he was married to three women at one time. However, Ndelekwa eventually married a fourth wife. When she gave birth to their first-born son, they named him Eliudi Ndelekwa Issanyga.

At Eliudi's birth in December of 1948, there were very few hospitals in the region. Babies were born at home with or without the help of midwives. If the baby was lucky enough to survive the birthing process, the parents sometimes took the baby to a clinic many miles away to receive what limited post-natal care that was available at the time. Eliudi would grow up with over forty brothers, sisters, half-brothers and half-sisters. However, some of those siblings would die during infancy or early childhood. Eliudi's age placed him about in the middle of that birth order. As Eliudi Issangya grew up on his father's farm, he tended the crops and watched over the family's pigs, chickens and goats.

In that area of Eastern Africa, the Lutheran religion had established many mission compounds and schools. Because of their influence, the farmers of Sakila considered themselves Lutherans as well. Even though that was their confessed religion, Martin Luther would probably not have recognized their life or worship style as conforming to his professed beliefs.

As Eliudi was growing to manhood, England awarded his country its independence in December of 1961. The new country was called Tanganyika. When the island of Zanzibar, which is off of the coast of Tanganyika, received it independence, the country of Tanganyika and the island of Zanzibar merged in 1964 to form a new country called Tanzania. The name was a melting of the words **Tan**ganyika and **Zan**zibar.

As a young man Eliudi naturally started to scout around for a suitable wife. In those days, the eligible men of a village would ride their bicycles or walk to a local town where they would gather to look over the eligible women hoping for the prospect of courtship and marriage. Eliudi was 21 years old when he hiked down the hill to a town 25 kilometers away from Sakila where he was going for a weekend visit at the home of an acquaintance of his.

On Sunday the youth of the village gathered for a party at his friend's house where music from vinyl records was played on a hand-wound gramophone. A girl named Helen, who was Eliudi's age, came to the party. Even though Eliudi talked with many people at the party, he was impressed with Helen and was attracted to her. The more he talked with Helen, the more he felt that she could be his wife. To further his interest in the relationship, Eliudi discovered that Helen also was a Meru and professed to be a Lutheran.

Both Eliudi's father and Helen's father were much respected clan leaders in the Meru tribe. That fact hastened the blessing of the parents concerning the marriage that Eliudi soon proposed with Helen.

With every African marriage comes the payment of the dowry to the bride's parents. Because the woman is considered a valued worker for the clan, the husband's parents must pay the bride's parents for loss of that worker and for the privilege of accepting the bride into the husband's family. The dowries usually included a cow, a few goats and whatever else the bride's parents were able to entice the groom's parents to add to the dowry to sweeten the deal.

The presenting of a dowry beef cow was not matter of simple delivery. In some cases, the animal had to be lead to the bride's village where it was slaughtered and butchered by the prospective husband. Then particular meat cuts and organs from the animal are delivered to certain members of the bride's family as determined by a prearranged plan. If an elaborate wedding ceremony was planned, the groom's parents must supply enough beef cows to feed all of the wedding guests.

Eliudi's parents gave Helen's family one milk cow, two sheep, two goats and some decorative blankets as the dowry. (The perceived value of the bride is measured in the number of cows awarded in the dowry.) After the proper dowry was awarded, Eliudi and Helen were considered properly married in May of 1969. There would be no public wedding ceremony or feast for them. The couple just moved in together completing the Meru process of marriage.

Eliudi's father gave the newly-wed couple four acres of his land. That amount of property was big enough to grow enough corn and beans to sustain a family and to have some surplus to sell at the markets in Arusha or in nearby Kikatiti. This small expanse of land also allowed some room to grow pigs. Eliudi's goats were herded with the other goats that belonged to some of his extended family members.

On this land Eliudi and Helen built a small two room house with the exterior walls being made of sticks and mud. In the middle of the living room was a place for the cooking fire and near it was a table. The other room was a bedroom that was just big enough for Eliudi and Helen's bed. The bed and furnishings in the house were given to Eliudi and Helen by his parents when they married.

It was later in 1969 that Eliudi Issangya accepted Jesus Christ as his personal Savior. His conversion story began in the city of Arusha, which is about thirty kilometers southwest of Sakila. One day while in that town on business, Eliudi heard the evangelistic gospel being preached for the first time by a group of native and Scandinavian people who were proselytizing and singing in an open area of the northeastern Tanzanian city. Even though Eliudi heard and understood the message about giving his life to Jesus, he did not fully accept it at first. His heart was willing to embrace the message but his mind was not ready to totally commit to it. As Eliudi went home to Sakila, he pondered what he had heard about God.

Over the next few weeks, Eliudi wrestled to understand what God's plan was for him. One day Eliudi walked from Sakila through the foothills of Mt. Kilimanjaro to the village of Kikatiti, which is four kilometers south of Sakila. When he arrived in Kikatiti, a public bus was barreling through the small settlement on the Moshi to Arusha Highway. To Eliudi's horror, a man about the same age as Eliudi stepped in front of the bus and was struck.

As the bus came to a screeching stop, Eliudi ran to the accident scene to see what he could do to help the victim of the bus collision. Unfortunately, the young man, who was still lying under the bus, was dead. Looking at the body, Eliudi heard the Holy Spirit talking to him saying, "What if you die suddenly like this man and you have not yet accepted the Lord? Here is a man, who is your age, lying dead. What if this had happened to you?"

The tragic situation really jerked Eliudi's heart. He immediately went to Arusha to seek out the evangelists that he had heard just weeks before. When he found them, he fervently asked for their prayers to help him to unconditionally accept the Lord as his savior. From that point on, Eliudi's life changed and God's will began to work in and through him.

When Eliudi's parents learned that he was confessing to be an Evangelical Christian, they rejected him and his wife for forsaking the tribal Lutheran faith. The professed Lutheran faith was, after all, part of the clan heritage. One day while Eliudi was away from home, his parents came into Eliudi's house and took back all the things that the parents considered to be their wedding gifts. His parents not only took the bed and table but also the dinner plates from the house. Without a bed, Helen and Eliudi were forced to sleep on a layer of banana leaves placed over the dirt floor.

The year after his conversion, Eliudi's farm grew and produced five times the amount of crops as it had the year before. Eliudi and Helen knew that bountiful harvest was from God. From the surplus of this plentiful yield, they were able to sell enough corn to replace the furniture that Eliudi's parents had taken from them. Eliudi also bought a little battery-powered radio so he could listen to the news being broadcast from Dar es Salaam. Eliudi and Helen felt really blessed by God for this miracle and expected that God would continue to bless their crops in this same way. However, Eliudi and Helen soon learned that the abundant increase of their crop yield did not endure on through the following years. Even so, their trust in God remained strong and they expected more miracles to happen at any time.

To this marriage, Eliudi and Helen's first-born son arrived in April of 1970. They named him Godwin Eliudi Issangya. All children born in the Meru tribe automatically receive their father's first name as their middle name. However when Godwin enrolled in secondary school, the registrar wrote down his name as Godwin Eliudi Selembo. Selembo had been his great-grandfather's first name. Since that name was written down on a formal document, it became his official name. Because giving the first-born child of a first-born son the grandfather's name is also an accepted practice in the Meru tribe, the mistake was not out of line.

CHAPTER 2:

YOUR LABOR IN THE LORD IS NOT IN VAIN

(1 Corinthians 15:58)

In the years after his conversion, Eliudi farmed his land and practiced part-time evangelism. However, the desire to preach God's gospel full-time was strong in Eliudi's heart. It seemed to Eliudi that as he farmed God was asking him if life was not more than mundane things like working, eating and drinking. Eliudi shrugged his shoulders at God and simply replied he did not know for sure what the purpose of his life was meant to be. However, he told God that he was ready to follow wherever He led.

One of the boys Eliudi grew up with in Sakila was John Mathew. John gave his life to Jesus about two years before Eliudi had. Even though John was a few years younger than Eliudi, they had a common Christian bond that cemented their life-long friendship. John and Eliudi would travel to the market places as a team to preach the gospel.

Even though, Eliudi wanted to preach the gospel full time, he still had to work on his farm. On a sunny, summer day Helen and Eliudi were working in the field on their little farm. As Eliudi looked up he saw a jet airplane passing overhead in the sky. Eliudi pointed at the airplane and said to Helen, "One day I am going to ride on one of those airplanes."

Helen shook her head and replied, "You should forget about that idea. We have work to do, so stop dreaming." Helen was sure that neither of them would ever be rich enough to fly in an airplane. Helen thought, "How could anyone dream of such an experience when you are not rich enough to have shoes to wear?" Eliudi laughed and pretended that what he had said was just a joke.

As more children were born into Helen and Eliudi's family, the offspring somehow found room to live in the two room hut. After Godwin, there were two girls born, Elizabeth and Rogathe. (Rogathe means "gift" in Swahili.) They slept in the common room of the hut and near the cooking fire.

The youngsters would sleep on cow hides spread out on the dirt floor. Since there were no blankets, the children kept warm by sleeping in their clothes.

In the mid-1970s Eliudi learned of evangelistic conferences being presented in Nairobi, Kenya and in Arusha and Dar es Salaam, Tanzania. With great anticipation, Eliudi, John Mathew and a number of their friends decided to attend the conferences. At those gatherings they heard numerous gifted and inspiring evangelical speakers.

In 1976 the Norwegian evangelist Amundsen was touring and preaching in Tanzania. He was also the founder of a well-known evangelism school in Norway. Eliudi was able to meet with Pastor Amundsen and to ask him questions about his work. As a polite joke Pastor Amundsen invited the inquisitive African to come to visit his school in Norway. However, Eliudi did not take it as a joke. He really wanted to see a ministry school and learn how it operated. Evangelistic education was something that he was truly interested in. Eliudi felt that learning at a school like the one conducted by Amundsen was the key to his spiritual growth and to understand how the gospel was best preached to unbelievers.

Eliudi gathered together some money by working part time jobs away from the farm. In October of 1977, he bought a one way airplane ticket to Norway to visit the Amundsen Ministry School.

His dream to fly in an airplane was going to come true after all. However, that did not mean that the first flight was not a major learning experience for Eliudi. When the airplane left the runway, Eliudi could not believe it when he saw the ground disappear from under the airplane. When the plane flew on for hours, he was sure that the plane would fall down to the earth at any minute. But it kept flying, finally reaching Norway.

In Norway, Eliudi was greeted by a very surprised Pastor Amundsen. Even if Eliudi was unexpected, he was soon given a tour of the school. Eliudi learned that the Norwegian school offered scholarships which included free room and board to worthy students. He also discovered that the classes were taught in English which Eliudi understood to a limited degree.

After the tour of the school was complete, Eliudi concluded that a visit just was not good enough for him. As a result, he submitted an application to study at the Norwegian school and was accepted. Fortunately for him, those classes started immediately. What started out on the surface as a short visit in Norway became a seven-month stay.

While one student attending the school was from India, Eliudi was the only person in the class from Africa. The remaining students were Scandinavian. Even with minimal language skills, Eliudi absorbed the evangelistic training like a sponge soaking up water. He closely observed the teaching techniques being used to educate and train the students.

Outside of class, Eliudi found that communicating with Norwegians was very difficult. However, what bothered Eliudi the most was the winter weather in Norway. It was the first time that he had seen snow falling from the sky. He became really concerned when the snow started to turn people's clothes white. "How could this be?" he thought. At first he felt very cold and shivered constantly from the freezing air. His new Norwegian friends noticed Eliudi's situation and quickly bought him some warm winter clothes to wear. Those new clothes helped some, but he still could not get warm. Because of the winter cloud cover, Eliudi became apprehensive when he did not see the sun for weeks on end. Even though people in Norway snow ski, Eliudi thought that sport too dangerous and cold for him to try.

After the class ended, the school staff paid for Eliudi's airline ticket back to Tanzania. Pastor Amundsen had taken a liking to Eliudi and, when in Tanzania, came to visit him numerous times in later years.

Back home in Sakila in 1978 Eliudi saw an advertisement in a Christian magazine about an organization in California that would provide Bible and evangelistic instruction, plus room and board, to qualified applicants at a school of ministry. The only cost to the students was that they had to provide their own way to the school in San Diego. That school was the Morris Cerullo School of Ministry.

Morris Cerullo believed that to spread God's message about Jesus Christ to the people in distant lands, the people who lived in those areas would have to preach it. In Eliudi's situation it meant that Africans would have to reach and teach their fellow Africans. To facilitate this type of ministry, Mr. Cerullo established a six month school in San Diego, California for Americans and foreign students to learn evangelistic techniques well enough to spread the gospel in their home areas.

Eliudi believed the advertisement in the magazine to be a golden opportunity opening for him. There were no schools in Tanzania where he could attend to learn how to evangelize Bible truths. He discussed with Helen his desire to become a full time minister for God. Afterward, he prayerfully applied for admission to the school in San Diego. The school received 80 applications from Tanzania and nearly 200 from neighboring Kenya. Eliudi was one of just two people selected from Tanzania. God blessed Eliudi, as He was aware of the vision in his heart and Eliudi's potential. Eliudi was notified of his selection and of the rapidly approaching date of the class.

The biggest obstacle to attending the schooling was that San Diego was half way around the world from Sakila. Eliudi wrestled in his mind with how he would pay for the airline ticket. No amount of part time work would accumulate the money he needed for an airplane ticket to America in such a short time. Eliudi's final desperate idea was to sell their farm's crop land. He would keep just the house and a partial acre of land for growing subsistence food for the family. The money from the sale of the farm land would be used to fly Eliudi to San Diego. Helen was not totally sure of this sale, but she trusted her husband and God to do the correct thing. After they agreed, Eliudi sold the farm land to one of his relatives to buy the one-way ticket to attend the ministry school. Eliudi's father was again infuriated with Eliudi for selling what basically was his inheritance.

In 1979 Eliudi flew to California leaving his three children and pregnant wife in Tanzania. However, US Customs required that if someone was coming temporarily into the United States, they had to have a round trip ticket home before permission would be granted to enter the country. After selling the farm, Eliudi had only enough money to buy a one way ticket. He took a giant leap of faith and flew to America anyway. Providentially, no agent of the Immigration and Customs Department even questioned Eliudi about possessing a ticket for the return trip home.

During his studies in America, Eliudi's English was at best questionable. The only English that he knew was what little he had learned in Tanzanian public schools. He had enough English skills to understand what he was being taught and to be barely understood when he spoke. His skill with the English language would constantly improve while spending time in America.

The Cerullo School of Ministry that Eliudi attended was six months in length. While at the school, God spoke to Eliudi about opening a school for potential ministry students in Tanzania. Because of poverty, many would-be-pastors in Tanzania were denied the chance to attend schools in Europe or the United States. The school that he contemplated would be accessible and free of tuition for those Africans choosing to attend. Of course, at this point Eliudi had no money to build a school and no land to build it on. But the seed was planted in his mind and it remained just a dream while he was studying at the Cerullo school.

Eliudi's first impressions of America were that the country was simply too big to be imagined. He was overwhelmed with what he saw. He got lost while walking the streets of San Diego. Eliudi would stand on a freeway overpass and look at all the automobiles and trucks going so fast below in opposite directions. He could not comprehend that each of those vehicles had a destination. He wondered, "Could there be that many places to go to in America?"

While Eliudi was in San Diego, his fourth child was born. It was quite a while before Eliudi found out about this blessed event as communication between Tanzania and America was not as rapid as it is today. Helen received little information from Eliudi during this time except for what written letters he was able to mail.

During the classes in San Diego at the El Cortez Center, the other students asked Eliudi about his life and future goals. When they found out that Eliudi had a wife and four children, they took up a collection for him. A member of the Mariposa Christian Fellowship by the name of Rocky Williams took Eliudi home with him one weekend. Rocky suggested to the church that they help support Eliudi while he was studying in the United States. A modest allowance of $50 per month was granted. In gratitude of the kindness, Eliudi named his newly born son after Rocky.

Another classmate who took a liking to this Tanzanian farmer was Helen Johnson. She was from Montana and sat in a desk next to Eliudi during the first day of classes. The students were then told that those seats would be their permanent seats for the entire training session. Eliudi talked with his classroom neighbor and discovered that her name was Helen. Since his wife's name was Helen, he felt comfortable talking to her. Over the course of the training, Eliudi talked to Helen Johnson a lot and they became good friends. Through Helen Johnson, Eliudi would make many contacts in Montana who would become instrumental in helping him later to build and develop his Bible school as well as other Tanzanian projects.

During this time in Sakila, Eliudi's wife and his children were having a difficult time surviving on the meager amount of crops that they grew. If the rains did not arrive at the correct time, the family would not have all the food that they needed. However in the African culture, the clan is set up so that all members will have their basic needs met if humanly possible. When one family is hungry, other families intervene and help out. This sharing of the surplus ensures that when a family comes up short on food, other families will pitch in and help them. Through this African social security practice, no family goes hungry even if the patriarchs of the tribe believe the hunger was caused by poor judgment.

Even though Helen and the children usually had enough food to get by, they did not have a cash crop to buy any of the other necessities that they required to make life easier. Times were hard for the family, but God made it work. During this time, nine-year-old Godwin learned how to become the man of the house and take care of his siblings and mother. He really tried not to become part of the problem, but to make things work. For Godwin this period was a learning experience for future times when his Father would be traveling away from home promoting the gospel and his school.

At the end of his ministerial classes in August, one of Eliudi's classmates provided him with the funds to buy a ticket to fly home. He went back to Tanzania with his dream to build the evangelistic school still beating strong in his heart. When he returned to Sakila, Eliudi expected that the Lord would immediately open doors for him to start building the school. But that did not happen, at least not right away.

After Eliudi returned home, he would tell Helen and his children some of the things that he had seen and experienced in America. To his son Godwin, Eliudi's description of the Cortez Center in San Diego sounded like heaven on earth. Godwin fervently wished that he could just see with his own eyes the marvelous wonders that his father had described.

All through 1980 nothing transpired to advance the construction of the evangelism school. Eliudi began to wonder if God really wanted him to start the school. Eliudi states of this period, "God has his timing and his people have to be ready at the correct moment to act. If God had inspired me to build a Bible school, then God's timing would be the best."

Some of his friends and extended family told Eliudi that his dream of a school simply was not going to happen. They asked him, "How can you teach, feed and house a hundred students who will be attending the classes twice a year when you have no land or buildings to work from?" But Eliudi had confidence in God and kept looking for opportunities to start God's school. During this time he was busy preaching the Gospel of Jesus Christ to all who would listen. One of his biggest and constant supporters was his friend John Mathew who soon shared the evangelism school vision. With Eliudi's help and guidance in 1981, John Mathew also attended the Cerullo School of Ministry.

The fact was that Eliudi's family was very poor. A lot of the time, there was no money to meet the many necessities of life. One day young Rocky rolled out of bed and landed in the cooking fire. He was badly burned on his buttocks. When this happened, Helen was at the market selling bananas to acquire some money to purchase food for the family. Eliudi was working part time at the Kilimanjaro Airport while it was being constructed and was gone for weeks at a time. The only adult in the neighborhood when Rocky was burned was the family's Aunt Vera. The other children went to her crying for help.

Aunt Vera did what she could to ease the pain of the burns. When Helen arrived back home, Vera and the kids were all crying because of Rocky's burns. Then Helen also started to hopelessly cry. Besides the fact that Rocky was severely injured, she knew there was not enough money to pay for medical care which Rocky required. (Helen had only gleaned enough money that day at the market for a one day's supply of food.) Since it was late in the evening, everyone tried to get some sleep until morning.

The following day Helen and Vera took Rocky to the hospital in Arusha where he received treatment for his burns. After he returned home, Rocky was still burnt bad enough that he could not sit down for two months. Eliudi's mother was the one who eventually paid Rocky's medical bills.

In the times that followed, there continued to be very little food for the family. The children would go to their grandmother and ask for food. Usually the grandmother gave them something to eat, but there were days when even she did not have any food. As bad as that was, this was the condition of most of the families in the village. It was normal to be hungry at times and you had to make do with what you had.

Eliudi's children did attended classes at the local public school. Since Helen was denied schooling by her father, she insisted that her children attend school. Because there was a fee for kindergarten, none of the kids attended that class. When the kids did go to school, they only had one set of clothes to wear. Sometimes they had no shoes and walked barefoot to school. Slippers were inexpensive so they were worn at times.

Many days Helen would be away from the house seeking part time work wherever she could find it. During those times, Rogathe had to stay home from school to take care of Rocky. Six year old Rogathe would clean the house, wash the dishes and clothes, and watch Rocky. When her mother got home, Rogathe would run off to what was left of the school day.

CHAPTER 3:

PREACH THE GOOD NEWS
(Luke 4:43)

With nearly no money, Eliudi prayerfully sought divine guidance on how to raise the needed funds for construction of his school. Eventually Eliudi felt that he needed to fly back to the United States where he would share his evangelism school vision with people that he knew there. In order to travel to the United States, Eliudi had to have a sponsor. The sponsor was required to write a letter to the State Department saying how long Eliudi would be staying and that they were totally responsible for him while he was here. The person or group of persons acting as the sponsor had to sign a form indicating that if the foreign guest should attain an un-payable debt of any size while in the United States, the sponsor would pay that debt in full. The sponsor also had to financially support the guest while he was here so that he would not enroll on government welfare.

Eliudi's sponsor would be the Mariposa Christian Fellowship in California. In December of 1981 when all of the forms were signed, Eliudi took another huge leap of faith and journeyed to America to first visit with that one small church in Mariposa. He would spend his first Christmas away from home with his friends at that church.

Even though the Mariposa Christian Fellowship wanted to assist in constructing the Tanzanian evangelistic school, they lacked the funds to support all of the building and operating costs of the school on their own. However, they did pray to God for more divine leadership for Eliudi. In addition, the church was able to assist Eliudi with a $100 a month living allowance while he was seeking finances for the school. It was time for Eliudi to travel on his own to look for other churches or individuals who possessed better prospects for additional financial backing.

Each year graduates of the Cerullo School of Ministry were invited to a reunion conference in California. While Eliudi attended the conference, he spoke to anyone who would listen about his vision. Because of his genuine and honest personality, he was able to receive support from three churches

- two from Oregon and one from Canada. Each of the Oregon churches gave $1,000 toward the ministry school. The Canadian church gave an additional $700.

A stranger at the conference gave Eliudi $1,000 and told him to "just go do it." That individual simply had enough confidence in Eliudi's vision that he was willing to help. Interestingly, that was the first and the last time Eliudi ever met that man. Altogether, Eliudi collected over $10,000 at the conference and from other contacts. Just as important, during those conferences and travels Eliudi started to establish a network of churches and individuals who were interested in helping him with his project.

Upon returning home in March of 1982, Eliudi had the capital he needed to construct the school buildings. The question in his mind remained – where was he to get land on which to build the school? John Mathew and Eliudi began to look around for available real estate. A promising parcel was found in Usa that would serve for the school. Usa is a town on the Moshi to Arusha Highway about half way between Kikatiti and Arusha. Eliudi and John worked for four months to complete the transaction. However, the government and some local individuals had some concerns about the school that probably could not be rectified. So that property was scratched off the list of possibilities.

When Eliudi arrived back in Sakila, he was inspired to visit his father, the very man who had strongly opposed his evangelical conversion just thirteen years before. Eliudi explained to his father about his vision of building a school of evangelism and how he felt that the vision was from God. Then Eliudi asked his father if he could buy some of his land in order to build the school. To everyone's surprise, his father approved of the project and freely gave Eliudi one acre of his valuable property. The only stipulation to the gift of the land was that Eliudi had to be successful. If he failed in his school endeavor, there would be no more help coming from his father - ever. If Eliudi's dream produced positive results, his 83 year old father said that he would consider giving him more help and additional land to expand his project.

As it turned out, Sakila was a very good place to build the ministry school. The scenery was lovely with Mt. Kilimanjaro to the northeast of the village. To the west was the impressive view of Mt. Meru and its volcanic crater. Additionally, the village of Sakila was wrapped around the northern base of Sakila Mountain. For the students the cooler climate of Sakila was conducive to study and learning about God. Mosquitos were seldom seen in Sakila. Plus, the campus was also a long way from any big city distractions. Except for the horribly rutted dirt roads to Sakila, the location could have been a good location for a resort.

After Eliudi acquired the land, he gathered a number of his friends and started to build the school. John Mathew was installed as second in command during the construction. Knowledgeable structural workers from Arusha were hired to direct the erecting of the school. The local people helped with the project but lacked the expertise to construct the cement block structures. All construction of the buildings was done by hand. One major problem encountered was the transport of building supplies to Sakila. The roads were so bad around Sakila that even the delivery trucks had a difficult time arriving there.

As lumber was needed for the construction of certain areas of the buildings, it was then that the homesteading location of Eliudi's father and his two uncles in Sakila became providential. Since the homestead was near the Arusha National Park, trees were readily available. The government had clear cut some pine-like trees from the park. Those trees had been sawed into lumber which was available not too far from the Sakila erection site.

Eliudi's son Godwin was drafted to haul water from a local swamp to the construction area. That water was hauled in barrels strapped to the back of the family donkey. The water was used for wetting the cement or mortar mixes and to water shrubs that were being planted around the property.

In December of 1982, the first four buildings of the evangelism school were completed. The finished buildings included areas for an office, a classroom, a dormitory, a cooking area and a dining room. The school became officially known as the School of Evangelism, but almost everybody called it Eliudi's Bible School. With the buildings complete, Eliudi had to face the realization that he had no classroom or office furniture. As a result, he went back to the United States to visit his supporters.

After a whirlwind of speaking engagements in America during the winter of 1982/1983, he was able to raise the funds for tables and chairs and other required furnishings. While visiting his former classmate Helen Johnson in Montana, an individual gave Eliudi $25,000 for the Sakila school. With those funds, Eliudi had enough to return to Africa to buy or build the furnishings that he needed. He even had enough money left over to buy six months' worth of food for the first class of students.

When Eliudi arrived in Bozeman, MT during that 1982/1983 trip, he gave a speech about his work in Tanzania and told of the dire needs there. One of the listeners at the house where the meeting was held was Betty Johnson. She was very impressed with Eliudi and his vision. In addition, Betty recognized that she had to introduce Eliudi to her sister, Clarice Wallin. Betty knew that her sister had a deep interest in the African people. Clarice had read many books on their culture and the conditions that they had encountered as a result of the slave trade during the 1700s and 1800s. When the introduction was made the next day, Clarice and Eliudi found they had a lot to share with each other. Clarice saw that Eliudi had a heart for God. Years later, Clarice said that during their first meeting she could "find no guile" in Eliudi as they talked.

The two talked long and intensely about conditions in Tanzania. As Eliudi spoke, one of the things that interested Clarice was the lack of clean water that was necessary for the daily use by the village and school. She was amazed that the people had to walk for miles from their homes with containers of water balanced on their head or strapped to the backs of donkeys to provide the water requirements of their families. She also learned that most of the water supply in Tanzania came from contaminated surface ponds, swamps or rivers.

Eliudi also explained to Clarice why he was in America. To facilitate the teaching process at the School of Evangelism, Clarice and her husband purchased a mimeograph machine and gave it to Eliudi. A mimeograph is a duplicating machine that makes paper copies of written, drawn or typed material from a stencil that is fitted around an inked drum.

In July of 1983, the school was ready to open. John Mathew and Eliudi walked around to the different churches in the area to let them know that their school was going to conduct ministerial classes in Sakila. The first class at the school included twenty students. The students who attended from northern Tanzania had a real hunger for learning how to spread the gospel.

In this class there was a man by the name of Amos Baruti. Eliudi saw something special in this student and, when he graduated, Eliudi asked him to stay on at the school as a teacher. Amos has been teaching at the School of Evangelism and pastoring a church in nearby Kikatiti ever since.

As word spread that a ministry school was established and operating in Sakila, opposition sprang up immediately to squash it. Many of the established denominational churches in northern Tanzania did not want an independent evangelism school in their area that was controlled by a native Tanzanian. Those denominations instructed their affiliate churches not to allow their members to attend Eliudi's school. As a result, the second class at the school had just two students enrolled.

At that point, Eliudi had a choice to make. He could close the doors of his long fought-for school or persevere and teach a six month class to the two enrolled students. Eliudi knew that this was a fight that had to be won. After a brief discussion with his school staff, the second class commenced with just the two students.

As the word got around about the quality of religious education being provided at the school, more applicants arrived to register for the classes. After that second class, the number of students enrolling at the school gradually increased.

The initial maximum number of students at the school was set at 100 individuals. The average class size during the years of 2000 to 2010 has been about 85 students per session. Some classes have had as many as 120 students enrolled while other sessions were attended by as few as 60. Living conditions at the school were modified to allow the new maximum number of students to be increased to 120.

In the African culture, a gift of money to a person for a specific purpose does not mean that the funds will go to that project. The usual thought process of native Africans is that any money on hand will go to the first financial need that arises, even if the money was given for a different designated cause. Westerners get frustrated when funds are donated for a project only to find that the money has been used for something else that seems unimportant and unrelated to their stated project. With that African practice in mind, westerners are reluctant to donate to projects supervised and operated by native Africans. In the case of the Sakila School of Evangelism, Eliudi was so focused on doing what God wanted him to do that all of the funding went directly to the building and operation of the school.

Even with the completion of the school, Eliudi's wife and children still lived in the small, two-room mud and stick hut. Many relatives chided Eliudi for not diverting some of the funds that he had received from America to build his family a nicer house. Eliudi would listen to none of that talk. He retorted, "The funds that I have received are from God and they will go to God's work."

Even though Eliudi had enough money to supply his first class of ministry students with food, he was worried about sustaining the subsequent classes. After discussing the situation with the other school leaders, it was decided that the school required some farm land to grow the food for the students. Seven kilometers southeast of Sakila, a 100 acre tract of farm land was found for sale. Using what money he had left from the building construction, Eliudi bought the acreage for $5,500. Hired workers were tasked with maintaining the farm. The school students were also pressed into the fields during planting or harvest time when extra hands were needed to work the land.

Eliudi's opposition troubles were not over when an adequate number of students enrolled at the school. With the school a growing success, a local man asserted that the School of Evangelism really belonged to him and that he had paperwork to prove his claim. That individual had helped early on with the school property and produced a deed with his name on it. With that in hand, he had the local police arrive and confiscate music instruments, sound systems and just about anything else that was not bolted down. However, Eliudi sued the man in a Tanzanian court and won back the school and its furnishings as a judge ruled that the man's claim was invalid. Needless to say, Eliudi has had to fight to maintain the independence and control of the school.

Each class session at the school is programmed to last for six months. The schedule is demanding and designed to produce dedicated evangelists. The students may not be Greek or Hebrew Bible scholars when they graduate, but they are ready to spread the gospel about Jesus. The demands on the students are great and not everyone who entered the opening classes completed the course.

People from various areas in Central Africa submit written applications to be accepted as a student at Eliudi's School of Evangelism. Some individuals have lobbied hard to be accepted at the school. Some travel to Sakila to meet with Eliudi to plead with him to be admitted. Most of the students are aware of the strict daily schedule that they will face before they arrive. As a result, the dropout rate has declined to nearly zero over the years.

As soon as the students arrive on the campus, they are introduced to a daily routine. At four o'clock in the morning, Eliudi rings a bell. If he is awake before then, the bell is rung as early as three o'clock. The "bell" is a sectioned truck tire rim that is beaten with a metal rod. This bell is the call to the students to gather for a prayer meeting. That prayer meeting continues until 5:30. Afterwards, the students have time to shower and eat breakfast. They then meet in the classroom for a chapel service at 8:00. From 8:40 until noon, the first formal Bible classes are conducted. From noon until 1 PM, the students have a lunch break. They then attend more classes until 3 o'clock in the afternoon.

After that point the students perform chores around the school. These chores include picking up debris from the school campus, cleaning the dormitory, gathering and splitting firewood or assisting with the cooking of the evening meal. Some of the students are engaged in maintenance of the various buildings or helping with the construction of different projects around the campus. From 4:30 to 6:00 they have personal time when they can wash their clothes, study or do other personal activities. Supper is served at 6 PM. From 7 PM until 9 PM the students are back in the classroom. They are supposed to be in bed by 9:30.

On Wednesdays, a prayer and fasting service is conducted at the church. All of the students take part in that weekly observance. The normal daily schedule is followed until 10 am. From 10 until 1, the students attend the prayer service. After a short break, the service continues until 3 pm. Then it is back to the regular schedule.

On Saturday, students have time to study their weekly lessons. If the school farm needs help, the students spend a portion of Saturday planting or harvesting crops. Sunday is spent at church with free time afterwards to relax and study. Many students meet at the church and hold an impromptu singing and praise service that can last for hours.

When the students have undergone three months of training at the school, they are given assignments to gain evangelistic experience. On weekends some of the students travel to open market places to spread the gospel and try to win converts. These markets could be in local towns like Kikatiti or in huge cities such as Arusha. Other students go to selected International Evangelism Churches where they join with a resident pastor to canvas the local area for converts or hold revivals at the church.

Once each training session, the students hike up Sakila Mountain for three days and two nights of fasting and prayer. As implied there is no eating or drinking during this time. Bishop Eliudi joins the students for this time with God. The days on the mountain are divided into segments. First the students pray for 30 minutes to one hour. Then they read their Bibles or nap for about two hours. Following that, one of the school leaders delivers a short message and provides the students with a topic to pray about. Among the things that they pray for are the school, Tanzania or their home country, American supporters, and the United States. They ask God to control all anti-Christian threats around the world so that the Gospel can be preached to all who want to hear it. With that task completed, the cycle starts over again. This sequence continues for the duration of the three-day fast.

Most foreign missionaries are aware that if the Gospel is to take root in people's lives, the individuals must have copies of the Bible written in their own language. In the beginning, some of the students that attended the school did so without a Swahili Bible. They had to borrow Bibles from other students who had brought their own. Meaningful study time was severely curtailed under those conditions. After the problem came to light, a number of churches in America bought 100 Swahili Bibles which were kept in a library at the school. From that stock of Bibles, a student could borrow one to read and study.

When a student graduates from the school, they receive a new Swahili Bible of their own as a reward. In America where we have lots of Bibles, this may not seem like a major event. However in Tanzania where many people do not own a single book, receiving a new Bible is a highly valued gift.

Historically speaking, 40% of the School of Evangelism graduates become pastors and religious teachers. 20% become traveling evangelists, while the remaining 40% are destined to become lay workers.

CHAPTER 4:
LET US NOT BECOME WEARY IN DOING GOOD
(Galatians 6:9)

In December of 1983, Bishop Eliudi was back in the United States. One of the first places he visited was his sponsoring church in Mariposa, CA. Eliudi and the pastor of the church went to congregational member Francis Kinley's home for supper. At that meal, Francis' son Garven and his wife Judy were visiting. When Garven met Eliudi, he felt God clearly telling him that he was going to be deeply involved with Eliudi's ministry. The problem was that Garven and Judy lived in Canada at the time.

In 1985, Garven and Judy decided to move to Mariposa. Two years later when the pastor of the Mariposa church resigned, Judy and Garven assumed the coordination of the American portion of Eliudi's ministry. Except for a short period of time when they moved back to Canada, they have been treasurers and communication coordinators for Eliudi's School of Evangelism, medical clinic, and orphanage.

Since the cost of shipping supplies and donations to Sakila is very expensive, that topic was brought up during Eliudi's 1983 visit. After some discussion, it was determined that a shipping container would offer a cheaper way of sending supplies to Tanzania. Even though the shipping of the container was expensive, it was still cheaper volume-wise than sending individual boxes. As a result a twenty foot container was obtained and parked at a site in San Jose, CA. Involved church members from around California and other states gathered to load materials in the container, which was later shipped to Sakila.

When the container arrived in Sakila, Eliudi's children found boxes addressed to them. In those boxes they found new clothes and shoes. The kids thought that that was really wonderful. They felt that their material life was finally getting better! They could go to church in nice clothes. When she was eight years old, Rogathe received her very first dress from one of those boxes. She remembers that the dress was red with a white collar. Before then she only wore a t-shirt or blouse with the traditional kanga. (A kanga is cloth wrapped around the lower part of the body to form a skirt.) Eliudi's family was somewhat concerned that the other villagers would be jealous of them because of their fine clothes and took humble measures so that others in the village would not be envious.

The well-being of the family started getting better with those gifts from America. Even though they missed Eliudi very much when he was absent, the children and Helen got used to him traveling to the States. For one thing, they knew that if he did not go, there would be no containers shipped with boxes of nice things to wear. And more importantly, they knew that he had to go to keep the supplies coming for his school.

Not only did the family received gifts from America, but the village of Sakila was bestowed with some much needed supplies. It was then that Eliudi's family realized what it was that Eliudi was doing for them and the village. The children became very proud of their father because of what he was accomplishing. They looked at the difference the School of Evangelism was making in people's lives through the tremendous and sacrificial efforts of their father. Even though the family had experienced hard times, they saw that God was leading their father and directing his vision. That vision was bigger than their needs.

In 1984 a man from Germany visited Sakila. In Eliudi and Helen's house he installed a methane lamp. It worked on the principle that animal manure, as it decomposed, would give off flammable methane gas. Near the house, the fresh manure was dumped into a pit that had a lid to cover and seal it. The gas was collected in the pit and piped to the lamp in Eliudi's home. The light given off by the lamp was equal to about a single candle flame, but it worked to produce free illumination.

Before the lamp was installed, the ministry teachers frequently visited Eliudi in the blackness after sunset. They would sit around in the dark and listen to news and programs from Radio Dar es Salam coming from Eliudi's old radio. Those radio broadcasts were a primary form of entertainment for the men in the village. While the radio was voicing the broadcast, the men would eat roasted corn-on-the-cob and drink coffee. After the lamp was installed the men could at least see each other without the use of a candle.

Since the lamp worked well enough, someone conceived the idea that the methane could be used to cook food using a small gas burner. A second pipe was connected from the line running from the pit to the newly installed gas burner. All worked well for a while. Then one day the burner for some reason blew up with a huge fireball. Needless to say that explosion startled Eliudi. Before nightfall, the burner and the lamp were out of his house. Eliudi decided that since he had someone who could gather firewood for his family, his household would return to cooking their food over a wood fire. With the use of candles and flashlights, the threat of exploding methane was eliminated.

Originally, there were only rudimentary roads and no electrical lines to Sakila. As time progressed, better roads were built to the village. That was followed by electrical power. With these physical improvements Eliudi had also brought spiritual hope to Sakila. One manifestation of that hope was that people started christening their children with Biblical names because of God's influence in their lives. For instance, names like Glory, Godlove, Godlisten and Agape became popular!

The mission campus in Sakila was in need of an automobile to pick up visitors from the Kilimanjaro Airport and to transport supplies from Arusha. The first car Eliudi bought was a well-used Land Rover that was purchased in 1982 with donated money. The purchase price for the Land Rover was $170. Eliudi was happy to buy the car as it was difficult in those days to find any vehicle to purchase in Tanzania. The Rover was purchased from a Canadian evangelist from the Assembly of God Church who was using it in the area northwest of Arusha. Luckily the Land Rover had four wheel-drive, which was a requirement because of the improving, but still difficult, roads around Sakila. Eliudi learned how to drive using that Land Rover.

The second-hand Land Rover was in questionable mechanical condition with even less than adequate brakes. It broke down at times while out on the road. A mechanic would have to be called from Arusha to fix the car as it sat alongside the road. Sometimes Eliudi would have to spend the night in the Rover waiting for the mechanic to arrive.

One day Eliudi was driving up the slope to Sakila when he did not successfully engage the transmission in a lower gear. The Land Rover lost momentum and started to roll backwards down the grade. Without good brakes, the car picked up speed as it bowled down the slope and went past Godwin who was tending the family goats alongside of the road. Eliudi did a masterful job preventing the Land Rover from wrecking. When the car came to one of the few flat areas, it rolled to a gentle stop. After a few thankful prayers, Eliudi knew that a newer and better automobile was mandatory.

In 1984 a Toyota pickup was shipped to Sakila from Montana. This pickup was to replace the tired, old Land Rover. Later in 1994, Leroy Snyder of Poulsbo, WA was in Sakila and doing some electrical work on the mission complex. When he saw the condition of the vehicles at the school, he journeyed to Arusha, bought a new Land Rover Defender from a dealer there and gave it to Eliudi.

That same year a supporter in Montana shipped a container to Sakila that contained a powered saw mill. This mechanism made expansion of the mission campus easier, particularly when it came to the manufacturing of dimensional lumber. That saw mill ran until it wore out in 2005. By then Marion Sluys of Poulsbo, WA had sent a replacement saw mill to Sakila. Since it was identical to the old saw, the original saw mill was used as a source of spare parts when the new mill had a break-down.

During this time, Bishop Eliudi continued to encourage supporters from America to visit his school campus. One couple from Montana who took Eliudi up on his invitation was Clarice Wallin and her husband, Norman. When they arrived at the airport, they were surprised to see that the entire school body, including teachers and students, had come to welcome them to Tanzania. Later in her visit she spoke to the students and said through a translator that she felt like she and her husband were coming home even though Sakila was a place they had never been. She felt the sincere love of the people toward her.

One of Clarice's fond memories was getting up at 4 AM in the cold African night to cook breakfast for the ministry school students. Not that cooking with a wood fire was all that enjoyable; the enchantment was that everyone who was cooking was singing praises to God as they worked. During her stay in Sakila, Clarice found that conditions in the village were exactly what Eliudi said they were.

By 1991 many western visitors were coming to assist Eliudi and his school. They thought that something should be done to move Eliudi and his family out of his old hut and into a nicer house. A pool of money was collected and the construction of the new brick house was started. The house was not only big enough to house Eliudi and his family, but starting in 1994 it also had guest-lodging for visitors staying in Sakila. That guest extension had a living room, two bedrooms and a bathroom with a shower.

After students graduated from the School of Evangelism, they journeyed back to their home areas. The original idea of the evangelical training was to educate the students and return them to their home churches to augment those congregations. However, when most of the graduates returned to their local churches, they were too spirit-filled to fit back into those churches. By 1986 they were being rejected by their home congregations in such a high number that the graduates had no place to go and returned to Sakila. Since these graduates had no legal footing to start new community churches, they were bewildered about where to turn next. Eliudi prayerfully decided that he should register a new church denomination with the Tanzanian government. It was a long laborious process, but in 1990, an application was approved by the government to officially establish the International Evangelism Church (IEC), with the School of Evangelism becoming the heart of the International Evangelism Centre.

Moses Mafie grew up in Sakila and knew Eliudi and his family. Even though Eliudi was older than Moses, they played and herded livestock together in the green valleys and forested ridges around Sakila. Later Moses would listen to Eliudi preaching in the village markets and was inspired by his messages. He became a born again Christian in 1992. In January 1993, Moses applied to study at the school in Sakila. After graduation, Moses spent six months evangelizing in cities in Kenya and Tanzania. In

December, Eliudi contacted Moses and asked him if he would like to teach at the school. After agreeing to the proposal, Moses started instructing in 1994 and has been teaching there ever since. He is now one of the leaders at the School of Evangelism.

Moses says that he has seen many miracles take place at the school. A few students come to the school with all sorts of burdens. Even with the aid of crutches, one student came to the school barely able to walk. During his study in Sakila, he was completely healed and walked home to Uganda without any help. Husbands who had been married for many years, but who had no children, were prayed for. God granted those families children after the student graduated. Moses has seen demons removed from students' bodies. Students are cured of alcohol and opium addiction. Those former addicts are now preaching the gospel of Jesus Christ and helping others to be free of their addictions. In addition Moses says that all students at the school receive healing to their souls.

A student, who also had the name of Moses, came to the School of Evangelism from his home in Morogoro, which is 190 miles due west of Dar es Salaam. Although he grew up in a Christian home, he later became a witch doctor. Remarkably when Moses was doing "the work of superstition," he heard the voice of Jesus calling to him to stop his heathen practices. Moses said the words sounded like thunder rolling across the sky. Soon after that God sent a messenger to Moses at his home to tell him about Jesus' love for him. After his life changing experience, Moses became a pastor of the gospel. Once his training at the evangelism school was complete, Moses planned to start a new church to save lost souls.

Another student by the name of Elia came from Tanga district in Tanzania. His story is remarkable in that he suffered major injuries inflicted by his father when Elia was just 12 years old. Both of Elia's legs were broken by his abusive father. Even though one of his legs was nearly cut off, Elia's father would not take his son to the hospital for medical care. Elia was left with leg damage that made it very difficult for him to walk. Later when Elia heard the gospel, he believed in Jesus. It was at that point that he cried out to his Savior and Jesus healed his crippled legs. "I will serve Him for the rest of my life, because of what He did for me," stated Elia. Elia heard about the evangelism school from a man of God and came to Sakila for instruction.

Every student who comes to the International Evangelism Centre has a story of the saving power of the Lord Jesus. Many, like Elia, have been healed of their afflictions either before coming to the school or while attending the training.

Early in 1992 Bishop Eliudi was visiting with and preaching at the churches in Montana that supported his mission. After touring the Mount Helena Christian Academy in Helena, he was struck with the idea that it would be a great high school for his third child, Rogathe, to attend. Eliudi asked the congregation of the Mount Helena Community Church if a family would like to host his daughter while she attended the school. Mike and Carla Kropp came forward to answer the call, feeling very strongly that the Lord wanted them to respond to Eliudi's request. The Kropps had two older sons and an adopted daughter by the name of Crystal who was just a year younger than Rogathe. Crystal was excitedly looking forward to meeting her new "African sister." She would also be instrumental in helping Rogathe through her cultural adjustment period in America.

Later in 1992, Rogathe completed her classes at the primary school near Sakila. Shortly afterwards Eliudi took her aside and asked her, "Do you know that you are going to America?"

Rogathe looked at him in amazement and asked, "What am I going to do in America? I am just 16 years old. How would I get there?"

Eliudi explained that she was going to Montana to attend a high school. He knew that she was a gifted individual and wanted her to have a good education. Then he told Rogathe that she was going to have to travel there by herself. No one could fly with her to guide her through the various airports.

Rogathe knew that she could not speak English. She wondered, "How am I to ask for help if I need it?" Eliudi said that he would write a note for her to carry. If she ran into any trouble, all Rogathe had to do was show someone the note and they would help her.

Eliudi had a plan to help Rogathe feel more comfortable about flying. She and Godwin would fly from the Kilimanjaro Airport to Dar es Salaam to acquire a visa for her to travel to America. On the appointed day, Rogathe took her first airplane ride. For her, flying was like sitting in a house that shook a little. Before the end of the day in Dar es Salaam, she acquired her visa. When Godwin took her back to the airport in Dar, he said, "I am not going to fly back home with you. You fly by yourself to prove that you can do it. I will take the bus home." After she landed at Kilimanjaro, Rogathe believed that she was ready to fly to America on her own.

Back in Sakila, Eliudi asked Rogathe if she could fly to America by herself. She answered that she could. He asked her the same question two more times. Rogathe said that indeed she was ready to go. She just pleaded with her father to remember the written note that he had promised to send with her. (Years later Rogathe would laugh and say the only thing that the note said was, "Please Help Me." And, that was all it said.) Eliudi also told his daughter that if she got into an uncertain situation at the airport where she was to change airplanes, she should find a person in a uniform to help her.

In early August Rogathe was put on a plane and her journey to America began. Indeed, she did require help at the first terminal where she had to change planes. She found a man in a uniform and asked him for help. Since he could not understand Swahili, the man looked at her ticket and motioned for Rogathe to follow him. There must not have been much time to catch the next flight as the man had her running through the airport to the proper gate. Rogathe was quite scared as nothing in her growing up years had prepared her for what she was experiencing.

Luckily, she had just one carry-on bag to lug around the airport. All she had in the bag were two pairs of shoes, two dresses and two winter coats. The coats were to ward off the cold in Montana. (Eliudi had tried to explain to Rogathe how cold it got in Montana, but she just could not comprehend such temperatures.)

When Rogathe arrived in America she had to board another airplane to Helena. A late night telephone call was placed to her host family from the customs officials located at the Atlanta Airport. The officer there wanted to know if they were expecting a visitor from Tanzania. After the Kropps replied that they were indeed aware of Rogathe's impending arrival, the officer then asked them if they knew that their visitor did not understand a word of English. This news came as quite a surprise to the Kropps.

Rogathe was becoming quite tired and bewildered from jet lag. Her days and nights were mixed up which resulted in her not sleeping on the airplane. Fortunately, she arrived at long last in Helena.

Rogathe's airplane touched down in Helena around 9 o'clock at night. When she got off the plane, all she saw was white people. She did not see anyone at all who had black skin. Rogathe was shocked at so many white people. Since this was not a bit like Tanzania, she was then even more alarmed than before.

Since it was late summer when she arrived, the cold weather had not yet started. Feeling the warm night air, Rogathe questioned in her mind why she would need the heavy coats that her father had sent along with her.

Mike and Carla Kropp, along with their daughter, Crystal, were at the airport to meet Rogathe and drive her to their house. Rogathe was immediately impressed with how nice the home was. She also noticed that there were no mud-and-stick homes anywhere to be seen in their neighborhood. To top all of that, she was given a bedroom of her own. Since her English was non-existent, the family explained in sign language how things worked about the house.

The Kropps assumed Rogathe must be hungry after such a long flight. They motioned with their hands to ask her if she wanted to eat. Rogathe managed to communicate that she was indeed hungry. Since it was late at night, they offered her a bowl of dry cereal. She had never seen a box of cereal before and did not know what to do with the box, bowl, spoon or gallon milk carton that was placed before her. At last she poured the milk into the bowl until it reached the brim. She then added ten Cheerios to the milk and began to eat. Lovingly, the Kropps showed her how to put more Cheerios in the bowl and then add less milk. Rogathe soon discovered that cereal was one of her newest favorite foods.

Then it was time for bed. Before she dropped off to sleep, Rogathe was overcome with the feeling that the Kropps were really nice people.

The next morning Rogathe experienced breakfast in America. The main item that she had for breakfast was black tea as she knew what that was. Hard boiled hen's eggs were something that she also recognized so she ate a few of those. She was hungry but, as the night before, she did not know what or how to eat most of the food that was placed on the table. In addition, Rogathe could not believe all the different types of breads that were served. Her African family had one type of bread and that was it.

It took Rogathe some time to grow accustomed to other foods that she was introduced to, especially Mexican dishes like enchiladas. However, she was willing to try almost everything and grew to enjoy a wide variety of cuisines.

Later on that first morning the Kropps took Rogathe shopping to buy her some clothes. Rogathe thought that the stores in Helena were a wonder to behold and that her new clothes were really nice. However, the one item that Rogathe questioned wearing was a pair of shorts. She had never been in public before with her legs exposed. Women in Tanzania almost always wear dresses or kangas which were long enough to cover their legs. At first, she would not wear the shorts, no matter how much the family encouraged her to put them on.

To have Rogathe meet some people her age, the Kropps went as a family to a Christian camp in late August. Also while they were there, they tried to teach Rogathe all the English that they could. Crystal and Rogathe would take long walks together with Crystal pointing at scenery or various objects. Crystal would say and repeat the names of the items so that Rogathe could learn a basic vocabulary in the month between her arrival in America and the time that their school would start.

As fall began to develop, the Kropps explained to Rogathe that she was scheduled to soon go to high school as a freshman. As a result, Mike, Carla, and Rogathe spent a day looking over the Mount Helena Christian Academy. At school the Kropps introduced Rogathe to her teachers. They welcomed her in English which she did not understand. Rogathe kept saying to herself, "This is bad. I cannot understand anybody!" The only people she felt that she could communicate with were her host family members, who spoke slowly and used sign gestures to help her understand.

After the phone call from Atlanta, the Kropps had anticipated the language problem and had bought Rogathe a Swahili to English translation dictionary. To understand what the Kropps were saying, Carla and Mike wrote down the English words and Rogathe would look up the words in her Swahili dictionary. That dictionary at least gave Rogathe the confidence to go to school.

The first day of school was not the most pleasant of experiences for her.

She was the only black student in the entire high school. For some reason, a few of the very young students at the school assumed that, since she was black, she did not take showers. When Rogathe understood what they were saying, she let it be known that she did take daily showers. To answer other student's questions, she would write down her answers in English.

On the second day of school, she was shown a desk to sit at and given some text books. Crystal took Rogathe in hand and led her around the school. She introduced Rogathe as "her sister from Africa." Even though Rogathe understood little of what was being said, she appreciated what Crystal was doing for her.

Rogathe was also amazed that Crystal had her own car to drive to school. After a while Rogathe believed that everyone in America had a car. America for her was an amazing place!

Later Rogathe wrote Crystal a note at school which stated that she was having trouble understanding the written English language. She requested that she be placed in a class with the younger children who were just learning to read English. Rogathe felt that if she attended those classes she could learn to read English faster. Then she could return to the high school classes to learn mathematics and other subjects. Math was something that Rogathe felt that she understood. Crystal talked to the school administration about Rogathe's request. They knew that something had to be done to teach Rogathe the required English.

So it was that she attended classes and learned to read about Dick and Jane. The younger kids loved to have Rogathe in their class and asked her many questions about Africa. From them she learned a lot of conversational English. Rogathe also prayed that God would help her to learn to read English in the shortest possible time. Within a few months after school started English began to come to her. Rogathe praised God for helping her learn the language.

Later, she wanted to sing in the school choir. The choir director wondered if Rogathe understood English well enough to sing it. Rogathe said if she could read English she could sing it. So she was accepted into the choir and was also given lessons on how to play the keyboard. The musical notes on the paper were easy for her to understand and follow.

One of the requirements at the school was that each student had to memorize Bible passages and to recite twenty verses each month. Soon Rogathe was memorizing English Bible texts with no problem. After two months, her Swahili dictionary was left in a drawer at home.

A teacher asked Rogathe one day if she could play basketball. At that time Rogathe did not even know what basketball was. She looked at the teacher and replied, "Of course, I can play basketball." As a result Rogathe came to practice every day and learned the game in a very short time. She played basketball so well that everyone believed that she knew how to play it before she arrived at the school. Rogathe also began to wear the dreaded shorts at basketball practices and games. She also started wearing shorts away from school during the summer.

Soon Rogathe learned the necessity of the heavy coats that her father Eliudi had given her. Winter sets in quickly and hard in Montana. Rogathe thought the cold was "crazy." One day she went to the front glass door of the house and saw white fluff falling from the sky. "What is this?" she wondered. Rogathe ran toward her sister's room and shouted excitedly for Crystal. Crystal came laughingly and informed Rogathe that what she saw was snow. Rogathe exclaimed, "In Africa we do not have snow except on the mountain tops!"

Then Rogathe quizzed Crystal, "Just how much of this snow is going to come down?" The reply was that the snow may continue for days or up to a week. She stared at Crystal in disbelief and said, "Are you joking me?" Crystal told her that it snows so much sometimes that they could not even go to school because snow became deep enough to clog the streets and highways.

Rogathe indicated to Crystal that she thought they were all going to die because of the snow. Crystal's response to that was, "Let us go outside and play in the snow!" It took Crystal some time to convince Rogathe to go outdoors with her. After the girls were dressed in their warmest coats, gloves and boots, they went outside where Crystal introduced Rogathe to snowballs. Rogathe had a lot of fun getting into a snowball fight with her American dad, Mike. In the weeks that followed, Rogathe learned to ice skate. She even learned to like the snow.

After the Kropp family vacationed in California, Rogathe was happy to get back to Montana where it was cooler. However, she did like California because the weather, plants and flowers reminded her so much of Tanzania.

Rogathe was careful to thank God for her successes. Occasionally she fasted three times a week to honor God's commitment to her, but she tried not to let the Kropps know that she was fasting. The Kropps, on the other hand, could not help but notice times when she refused food. Mike and Carla respected her wishes during those episodes.

Mike and Carla Kropp fell in love with Rogathe and still consider her their daughter from another family. They and their daughter, Crystal, consider her as one of the greatest gifts that God has ever bestowed on them.

Between Rogathe's junior and senior year of high school, the Kropp family had to move away from the Helena area. As a result, Ron and Cathy Gipe became Rogathe's host family. With that move came a new high school. So it was that in May of 1996, Rogathe graduated from Flathead Christian School in Lakeside, MT.

When Rogathe graduated, she flew back to Tanzania. Rogathe's American sister, Crystal, traveled with her and spent several weeks with Rogathe's family. For her part, Rogathe was ready to return home to the simpler life in Africa. After living in Montana during all of her years of schooling, Rogathe was worried that Tanzanian weather would be too hot for her. However, she soon discovered that she fit right back in her African home. Years later, Crystal would again travel to Tanzania with her husband, David. Mike, Carla and Crystal remain actively supportive of Eliudi's projects and try to visit with Eliudi every year when he comes to America.

Eliudi's oldest son, Godwin, had also traveled to America for his education. His story will be told later. Elizabeth was Helen and Eliudi's second born child who was schooled in America as well.

CHAPTER 5:
BUILD ON THE FOUNDATION WITH JESUS AS THE CHIEF CORNERSTONE
(Ephesians 2:20)

As the School of Evangelism in Sakila grew, a quicker means of tilling the ground at the farm had to be found. A farm tractor and plow were bought to mechanize the growing of the crops. After the land was tilled, the plow was left at the farm while the tractor was stored at the school. (Today, most farmers near Sakila still use oxen and wood framed plows to till their fields.)

A few people were hired to work the school's farm including a man who was Helen's younger cousin. One day the cousin came running out of breath into Eliudi's home exclaiming that the plow at the farm had been stolen. Eliudi knew his junior cousin-in-law like he was his own son and told Helen that he believed that her cousin had something to do with the disappearance of the plow. Eliudi looked the young man in the eye and said, "Tell me where the plow is." The cousin insisted that the plow was stolen and that he had nothing to do with its disappearance.

With no confession coming from the cousin or anyone else, an inquiry for the missing plow commenced. The search was conducted for 17 days without discovering a single, possible clue as to where the plow was hidden. This plow would be expensive for the Bible School to replace but essential for the student's food production. Finally Eliudi publically proclaimed that he and the school leaders were simply going to pray for the safe return of the plow and for God to take care of any punishment of the thief. There would be no more searching; they would just pray and leave the plow in God's hands.

On the eighteenth day after the plow disappeared, a man came to Eliudi to ask him if he had recovered his missing plow. Feeling a bit perplexed about the question, Eliudi hesitantly said, "No." The man then informed

Eliudi that he understood that the plow would be transported to Arusha and sold on that very day. The man also said that if Eliudi would hurry to a certain farm near his school's farm, he could find the plow which had been disassembled and hidden.

Eliudi and the school leaders notified the police of the tip and asked the police to meet them at the designated farm. When everyone was assembled, the search for the plow commenced. At first they looked in the house and out buildings for the plow, but found nothing. Eventually, the plow was discovered disassembled and buried in three separate pits.

When the plow was recovered, the cousin confessed to the crime. No legal punishment of the cousin was administered. Eliudi just fired him from his job at the farm and let him go on his way.

Each year Eliudi traveled to America to visit his supporters and tell them of the progress being made in Sakila. On some of the trips, his wife Helen would travel to the United States with Eliudi. These trips were not a vacation from the school for Eliudi. Clarice Wallin relates how Eliudi spent his time with her and Norman in Bozeman, MT during one of his stays with them. Eliudi would get up at 4 o'clock in the morning and spend hours in prayer. Later, he would speak to Clarice's morning Bible study class. She remembers one memorable talk that Eliudi gave by holding a US coin and pointing out the words "IN GOD WE TRUST." Eliudi then talked the entire Bible session on that topic and read passages from the Bible on trusting God.

Eliudi was also featured on the local Christian radio station in Bozeman and was a guest speaker at area schools. Local doctors and nurses also came to hear Eliudi speak about the medical needs of the people of Tanzania. Many doctors said they were impressed with Eliudi's practical vision of the medical work that needed to be accomplished in Africa.

Each year after 2004 when Eliudi visited Bozeman, there would be a dinner given in his honor. This dinner was attended by people from various churches in and around the Bozeman area. After the dinner and a speech given by Eliudi, a cake and memorabilia auction would be held to raise money for Eliudi's various African concerns. Clarice would donate to the auction African cloth, wooden animal figurines and other things that she had collected on her one visit to Sakila. Since these items came from Clarice's personal collection, she was reluctant to part with them but did so to support Eliudi. One year enough money was raised to buy the school two photocopy machines to replace the mimeograph machine that Clarice had given the school so many years before.

Of course, visiting the Wallins was not all work. According to Clarice, Eliudi loved to go shopping at Costco. Even if he did not buy a thing, he just enjoyed looking at the stacks of merchandise and food that were available. Eliudi's African mind had difficulty comprehending so much food in one place. One of his favorite foods was peanut butter. Eliudi was amazed at all the huge jars of peanut butter that were on the store's shelves. Each year when the mission workers would ship boxes of essential supplies to Sakila, Clarice made sure that a case of peanut butter was also included for Eliudi.

One of the things that amused the Wallins was that Eliudi used a lot of sugar in his coffee. And when he drank coffee, it had to be boiling hot. When Eliudi ate at a restaurant, he would have the waitress repeatedly microwave his coffee to keep it near the boiling point.

Clarice Wallin continued to actively support Eliudi and his ministry until she turned 95 years of age. At this writing, Clarice is still living in Bozeman and speaks highly of her times with Eliudi and Helen and of Eliudi's work in Africa.

Early in the 1990s a young woman by the name of Enekia came to Sakila looking for work. She knocked on Eliudi and Helen's door and asked them if they had need for a domestic servant. Even though they hired her as a housekeeper, she soon became part of the family. In 1994 Enekia left Sakila to go back to school in Dar es Salam.

While Enekia was attending school, she met a lady by the name of Lucy. Mama Lucy had been widowed in 1997 and was temporarily living in Dar with her two sons. Lucy became a born again Christian in 1999 and attended the local Assembly of God Church. At that church she met Enekia who was a prayer group pastor. Lucy was so impressed with Enekia that she informally adopted Enekia as her daughter. Enekia would come and stay at Lucy's home for up to a week. They spent many hours in prayer together and enjoying each other's company.

(Every woman that is well respected in Tanzania is called "Mama." This shortened title comes from the Swahili word for "lady" – akina<u>mama</u>.)

At that time, Lucy's brother was an executive pastor at the International Evangelism Church in Dar es Salaam. That church was quite a distance from Lucy's home, but she went there when there was a crusade. At one of those meetings, she was able to hear Bishop Eliudi speak.

At Lucy's church there was a small group of men and women who had recently lost their spouses. To ease the grieving process, the pastor of the small group encouraged the female members to buy a man's shirt of the size and color that they liked. (The men in the group bought blouses of the size and color that they liked.) The theory went that if God wanted them to marry again, the person that God intended for them would fit that shirt. The small group members brought those shirts and blouses to church where they were prayed over for a week. Later, Mama Lucy hung that shirt in her closet at home. It hung there for six years. Sometimes she would try it on and think about a new husband to wear the shirt. However most of the time, she would just forget about it.

It was after meeting Enekia that Lucy moved to Mozambique with her two sons. Lucy's husband had been a citizen of Mozambique all of his life. There Lucy started a successful small business in the capital city. Since she was living a comfortable life, Lucy was happy residing in Maputo. She had no intention of moving back to Tanzania. Enekia came to that country often to visit with Mama Lucy.

As Eliudi received more donations from America, he wanted to start building projects to enlarge the School of Evangelism campus. A large hall had been built to have a meeting place for the yearly, week-long graduate conferences. However, the graduates soon returned in such a number that the group was too large to be housed in the building. As a result, the gathering was held outside of the hall. Not only were the graduates of the school returning but they were bringing their families and church members with them to hear the inspired preaching. The building that had been erected with the capacity for 300 people was simply too small.

Eliudi's father had died in 1984. However he saw that the school might be a success and would possibly need land to expand. Before he died he gave some instructions to his third wife, Masira, who owned the property surrounding the one acre school campus. He made a verbal agreement with her that if Eliudi ever needed more land; she was to give it to him. What made this feasible was that Masira did not have any male children. As a result she had no descendants that could inherit her land. The agreement between Eliudi's father and his third wife stipulated that if she gave the land that Eliudi needed to his ministry, she would become Eliudi's adopted mother. Since she would be his second mother, Eliudi would then take care of her for the rest of her life.

As a result when it came time to expand the campus, Eliudi received thirteen more acres for his use. There was no written will for this land transfer, just a verbal covenant that was honored. If Eliudi's father had not arranged this agreement with Masira many years before it was needed, expanding the school campus would have been very difficult, if not impossible. God had opened this door before it was even recognized that the need was there. (Masira died in 2012 at the estimated age of 102.)

Tanzanian coffee is recognized as some of the best grown in the world. Every day at 4 PM, a coffee break is held where the school leaders, teachers, workers and important guests can sit on benches and drink the local coffee, sweetened or unsweetened. Bishop Eliudi makes it a point to attend all of these daily afternoon breaks.

One day in 1992 during the afternoon coffee break, Eliudi was relaxing with Godwin and others while quietly discussing the day's events. However, everyone was watching Eliudi who had a hammer and four wooden stakes in his hand. When the social time was about over, Eliudi asked all in attendance to follow him to a large open area on the west side of the fourteen acre school campus. Eliudi stood at one corner of the vacant area and hammered a stake in the ground. At that point, nobody knew what Eliudi was doing. He handed one of the stakes and the hammer to his son Godwin and told him to walk in a certain direction. Godwin took thirty steps away from his father and stopped to look back. Eliudi told Godwin to keep walking. Each time Godwin would stop and look toward his father, Eliudi would laugh and say, "Keep walking. Just keep walking."

When Godwin was about 150 feet away, Eliudi told him to hammer the stake into the ground. Since the distance was so far, those who were watching the proceeding were thinking that Eliudi was staking out a new bean or corn field. Eliudi was enjoying the look on the faces of his observers and finally said, "Gentlemen, this is going to be our new conference hall." The dimensions that were staked out were huge. Nothing like it had ever been built in Sakila and that caused all those in attendance to chuckle out loud. The dimensions of Eliudi's building were just too outrageous for the men to believe that Eliudi could be serious.

To prove that he was serious about the building project, Eliudi started the foundation for the conference hall that year without having nearly enough money to complete the construction of the building. Plus, there was no avenue at that point to acquire the additional money to finish the building. Constructing the hall was going to be a faith builder for those who worked with Eliudi.

The new hall's footing area was excavated by hand with rocks laid in the trench for drainage. To gain some much needed construction funds, Eliudi sold some land that he had previously acquired. Fortunately it was discovered that the Tanzanian military needed some lumber at that time. Since Eliudi had a saw mill, he traded cut wood for the engineering design of the hall. This design work came along with some much needed military manpower.

When the concrete foundation was poured and back-filled with dirt, the soldiers moved to the campus on weekends and were housed in one of the evangelism school buildings. The soldiers, who are like America's Army Corps of Engineers, worked hard and did a marvelous job of erecting the walls of the new conference hall. With the walls finished, all that was required was a roof to complete the structure.

In 1996 while Eliudi was in the United States, he bought a Toyota Four-Runner and had it shipped in a container to Sakila. When the automobile arrived, Eliudi drove it to a Muslim contractor, who was a friend of his. Eliudi indicated that he would give the Toyota to the contractor if he would design a roof for the hall and have his work crew install it. The man looked the car over and quickly agreed to do the work. The Muslim contractor knew of the good deeds that Eliudi was doing for all the people of Tanzania and wanted to help him in return. Eliudi received a $30,000 roof for the price of a $14,000 car.

Since the width of the hall to be spanned was 94 feet, the roof had to be specifically designed for the conference building. In addition, Eliudi did not want any support columns in the seating area to block anyone's view of the stage at the front of the hall. The contractor designed a metal rafter system to hold up the roof and safely span the distance. After the design was complete, the rafters had to be custom-manufactured. The contractor's workers then arrived in Sakila and installed the trusses and roofing material.

The conference hall took more than four years to complete, but it was finally finished and ready for use. Not only was it used for the returning graduate conferences, but it was also used for community functions as well. The new hall worked so well that it became the church building for the people in the Sakila area.

Besides the church/conference hall that was built in Sakila, another church building was desired to be constructed in Arusha. Years earlier, a formal ministry center to help coordinate Eliudi's projects was planned in Poulsbo, WA on some land donated to the ministry. However, the land-use permit was rejected by the Poulsbo city planners. That land was subsequently sold with the selling price donated to IEC in Sakila. With that money in hand, property was sought for purchase in Arusha.

IEC had a presence in all the major cities in Tanzania except Arusha which was the biggest city near Sakila. Eliudi and the School of Evangelism leaders prayed to God for guidance to find a large parcel of land on which to build a church in that city. They estimated that they would need more than ten continuous acres to complete what they had planned. After examining the land for sale in Arusha, they discovered that there were mostly just small lots for sale. Those lots were just large enough to accommodate the building of a single house.

Eliudi left the problem of buying the real estate in Arusha to an evangelist that he knew in the IEC church. Eventually the evangelist found a large, 12-acre parcel of land that would meet the church's needs, but the Christian owner had sub-divided the parcel into lots and only wanted to sell the land one piece at a time. By selling the land in that fashion, the owner would make more money. When the evangelist begged the man to sell the entire property to his church, the owner flatly refused to listen to the request.

A week after the refusal, the evangelist was inspired to go to the owner's home late in the evening and knock on the land owner's door. The land owner was not happy about being awakened and demanded to know why the evangelist was there. The evangelist told the owner, "Let us sit down and I will tell you why I am here."

When the two were sitting in the man's living room, the evangelist explained, "God has sent me here. I believe that God wants you to sell your land to the church. But if you do not, I will just leave. I will not come back to bother you again." The land owner was a bit apprehensive that if he denied the offer, God may not bless his proposed land sales. After some thought, the land owner changed his mind and sold the land to IEC.

However, the man had already sold two lots of the land to other individuals. He was not sure how he would rectify that situation. The evangelist suggested that the man call on the people who had bought the lots and ask them to give it back as the church wanted to buy the land. The land owner indicated that he thought that probably would not work but he would try. When he visited the two buyers the next day, he explained the situation to them and offered to give back their money which they had paid for the land. Surprisingly, both lot owners agreed to tear up their deeds if they got all of their money refunded. Soon after that, money was transferred to the land owner and the property came under IEC control.

On that land, a church building was designed and constructed to provide the larger IEC presence in Arusha. That church was constructed in 2002. Since then the church has become a huge part of the community. The church even has a well that provides water for the local residents. To give the local children of Arusha something to do, a soccer field was also laid out on the church property.

Both the Sakila and Arusha churches are ministered by IEC pastors. Eliudi does not pastor either church but does supervise their activities. When Eliudi is in Tanzania, he takes his turn preaching at the churches.

About one hundred yards north of the Arusha church, IEC built an orphanage. The orphanage was started by an American who had a vision for parentless children of Tanzania. With AIDS infecting nearly 6% of the population of Tanzania, many children are left homeless by the disease. (Approximately 44% of the children at the orphanage are there because their parents have died of AIDS.) After a dormitory building was constructed, the first 20 orphaned children were admitted. The original plan was to have as many as 200 orphans at the facility. At this writing, there are currently around 50 children living at the orphanage. Its official name is Christ Hope Orphanage.

From that original starting point, other individuals have stepped forward to fund and support the orphanage. In America, a sponsorship program has been set up to meet each individual orphan's needs. Since these orphans are children, they receive care 24 hours a day, seven days a week, from a staff of eight adults. The children are housed, fed and given medical care. When a child is ill, an adult will take the child to a local clinic for treatment. The children at the orphanage attend the local public school and are required by the government to wear a uniform which is purchased with sponsorship contributions.

Since its start-up, more buildings at the orphanage have been constructed. There are now four dormitory rooms, two for girls and two for boys. Full-time dorm mothers and fathers have been hired to live with the children to monitor and care for them.

When the children come to the orphanage, they may have had secular, Muslim or tribal names. Those are the names that the kids were enrolled under at the public school. The children are taken to church once a week and received Christian teaching during the evenings after school. The public school officials came to the orphanage one day and wanted to know who was forcing the kids to change their names. The kids in question were interviewed by the school officials and they explained that they themselves had changed their names. They stated that they were following Jesus's example and wanted names that were Christian. In their viewpoint, since Jesus cared enough for them to provide them a place to stay and food to eat, they wanted to have names that Jesus knew. So now there are kids at the orphanage who have new names like Angel, Miriam or Joshua.

To be sure, the land purchased in Arusha is not in the best neighborhood. A God-led organization builds churches where the most potential converts are. But, as a consequence of the unsettled neighborhood, the pump in the water well has been stolen twice. The thieves break off the top of the well casing and pull the pump and pipe from the well to sell them on the recycle market. A water pump with its motor could bring as much as $1,000 to the crooks. If the thieves loosen the pump and piping from the well outlet fitting from which they are suspended and accidently drop them in the well, the well becomes worthless unless the pipe and pump are retrieved and set back in the well properly. That is exactly what happened during the third attempt at robbing the pump from the well at this site.

The internal pipe was loosened from its outlet fitting, but then the whole mechanism was dropped into the well when the thieves lost control of the pipe and pump. If the pipe and pump could not be removed, the well would have to be given up for lost and a new well drilled. Since well driller Trusty Matheson from Wyoming was not in Tanzania at the time, Charles, a member of the drilling crew, would have to try to retrieve the pump. Eliudi prayed with Charles, "Lord, we do not even know how to do this job. But we must save the well because the orphans and the community rely on this water. Give us wisdom on how to do this. Amen."

The only thing that Charles knew was that Trusty Matheson called the retrieval of the lost pump in a well as "fishing." Since Charles had fished in a river before, he built a large metal fish hook which he planned to lower into the well, snag the pipe and pull the pump back into place. He believed that they had just a 50% chance of ever succeeding in retrieving the pump.

As Eliudi prayed to God at the well site, Charles lowered the home-made fish hook using a rope into the well. On the very first try, he snagged the pipe top and was able to pull the pipe and pump back into its proper position. Water could once again flow for the neighborhood. Everyone was shouting, "Halleluiah!"

CHAPTER 6:

HE SENT THEM OUT PREACHING THE KINGDOM OF GOD

(Luke 9:2)

Eliudi Issangya has received numerous honors over the years. Many Tanzanian officials have visited his campus in Sakila to show the government's appreciation for the good that Eliudi has accomplished.

Most Christian churches in Tanzania have leaders who are commonly known as bishops. It is these bishops that the national government contacts for guidance when a need arises that concerns the religious community. However, the International Evangelism Church did not have bishops in its administrative structure. Since IEC was a growing member of the East African Christian community, Eliudi was designated by his organization to be IEC's bishop. In December of 1994, the President of Tanzania was scheduled to attend the ceremony that acknowledged Eliudi as IEC's bishop, but because of a political crisis, the President was not able to attend.

At times there are as many 100 Christian leaders in Tanzania with the government-recognized title of "bishop." From these individuals, eight or ten are selected by the body of designated bishops as lead bishops to be representatives to the government. Eliudi Issangya is one of those. However, the position of bishop is more than an honorary title. When there is national need for Christian direction during a calamity, those lead bishops are called to mediate various situations.

As an example, in October of 2012 two boys in Dar es Salaam were discussing their religions as they believed them to be. One boy was a Christian while the other was a Muslim. The Muslim boy stated that if someone desecrated his Koran, Allah would turn that person into a wisp of smoke and his life would be over. The Christian boy said that he did not believe that was true at all. To settle the matter, the Muslim boy put his Koran on the ground. The Christian boy then urinated on the book. Sure enough, the Christian boy was still alive, but the Koran was trashed. The Muslim boy took his ruined Koran and told his father about the incident. The

Muslim boy must have been questioning his father about what he had been taught. However, the father went to his local Muslim leaders and related what had happened.

Instead of the incident being between two boys exercising their faith, it now became a volatile situation. Riots erupted in the streets with armed gangs of Muslims and Christians confronting each other. A few Christian churches in Dar es Salaam were burnt to the ground. To quell the hostilities, the national government called in the Christian bishops to mediate the situation with the Muslim leaders. As part of the team, Eliudi was invited to Dar es Salaam (which means in Arabic "haven of peace"). Eliudi and his fellow bishops stood up for the rights of the Christians, deplored the burning of the churches, and worked to bring about peace. After three days of meetings, tension was reduced between the two religions to a point where a shooting war was not going to start. When Eliudi returned home to Sakila he was mentally exhausted.

After a few years, the students at the Bible School were not just arriving from Tanzania. They came from numerous countries in the area such as Congo, Burundi and Rwanda. Eliudi began to think it was advisable that he should start schools in those countries so that students would not have to travel so far to attend classes in Sakila.

A graduate of the Sakila School of Evangelism had started a ministry school on his own in the Congo. Similar to Bishop Eliudi's vision, that student felt that God wanted him to build a school for prospective pastors in his country. He operated the school in the Congo for nine successful years in some very difficult situations. As the Congo school grew, that individual asked Eliudi's staff for assistance in administrating the school. After a review of the work being accomplished in the Congo, the school was placed under IEC oversight in 1994. That school has prospered and is now an important part of IEC. Along with other projects, a Congo orphanage is being built there as well.

It has been Eliudi's management style to trust those who are put in charge of various IEC projects. He knows that there is no way he could manage the everyday operations of all of his various interests. He trusts in God to lead those he leaves in charge of the varied projects.

Recently, an unusual function was assumed by the School of Evangelism leadership. The school staff is now protecting and housing native albinos at the school. Statistics show that worldwide, about one in every 20,000 babies born will be an albino. In Tanzania that number is one in every 1,400 births. In Eastern Africa, some witchdoctors came to believe that if they and their followers devoured albinos, they would receive magical powers. As hard as it is to believe that cannibalism is still practiced today, albino individuals were being murdered and eaten. Between 2006 and 2012, 71 albinos have died in these attacks. To guard those white skinned Tanzanians, personal protection and housing was offered by the school.

While on a trip to the United States in 2007, Eliudi and Helen made the rounds visiting their supporting churches. When Helen arrived in Poulsbo, she was not feeling very well. Her son, Godwin, took her to a local doctor's clinic and it was discovered that Helen had diabetes and needed insulin injections to control the disease. Those injections controlled the diabetes fairly well and she felt fine for nearly a year.

In 2008 Helen started to have other medical problems. She would eat very little as she felt full after ingesting just a few bites of food. Even though she was not eating, her abdomen was progressively swelling. Helen was taken to various clinics in Arusha to diagnose the problem. It was discovered that her body was retaining fluids. Even though medications were administered to her to remove the excess fluids, her health did not improve. She got to a point where she had to have assistance to stand up or move about her house. While Eliudi was traveling, Helen's children did what they could to assist her. Enekia, the former housekeeper, also returned from Dar es Salaam to stay with Helen for two months. Godwin flew to Tanzania from Seattle five times in 2009 to assist her. Even though Helen was placed in the Arusha hospital, the doctors in Tanzania never found out what was wrong with her besides the diabetes.

Before Bishop Eliudi left in December 2009 to come to the United States, Helen was once again placed in a hospital located near Arusha. This hospital was a new facility built by a group of German Lutherans, located near

Mt. Meru and having a reputation for giving good medical care. The doctors there looked for the right combination of medical diagnosis and treatment. In January 2010, Helen took a turn for the worse and was placed in intensive care. A phone call was made to Eliudi that his wife was near death and that he should return home immediately from America. However before he arrived home, Helen died on the second day of February.

With all the children assembled in Sakila, Eliudi planned the funeral for his wife. The service was held at the church in Sakila and was attended by seven thousand people. Religious ministers representing different churches from many kilometers around came to the service. Also, national politicians came to pay their respects. So many mourners arrived that twelve police officers were dispatched to Sakila to direct automobile traffic. A police escort was obtained to bring Helen's body from Arusha to the church in Sakila for the funeral. Never before or since has there been so many people in Sakila for a ceremony.

After Helen's funeral, Eliudi realized that he had never been in charge of the International Evangelism Centre without Helen's help to run their home, crop land, garden and personal farm. The Bishop's wife had also been responsible for supplying and overseeing the cooking of the meals for all western visitors who were in Sakila at the IEC campus. Things began to deteriorate at the house where Helen had lived. Even with the domestic help that Bishop Eliudi employed, things were becoming unmanageable. In addition, those domestic servants needed supervision and direction. Enekia stayed with Eliudi for a month after Helen's death to assist around the home, but even she had to return back to her home on the coast.

When Enekia returned to Dar es Salaam, she then made a trip to Mozambique to visit Mama Lucy. Enekia would talk about the Sakila family and how nice they had been to her. Lucy admired Bishop Eliudi and his family from what Enekia was telling her about them without personally having met them. Enekia expressed her desire that Mama Lucy would someday meet Bishop Eliudi as both were devout followers of God.

One day during her visit, Enekia was talking to Bishop Eliudi on her cell phone and could tell that he was missing his wife very much. Enekia asked

Mama Lucy if she would speak a word or two to Eliudi to cheer him up. Lucy said that she did not know Bishop Eliudi but she would speak some sympathetic words to him. As a result she took the phone and gave him some encouragement. That was the first time Lucy and Eliudi had talked to each other.

On a day in 2010 Enekia called Lucy from Dar and asked her to come to visit her. Enekia wanted to take Lucy to pay condolences to Bishop Eliudi in Sakila. Lucy said, "Sure, someday we will do that. We can't do that now because I am on my way to India to visit my youngest son who is going to school there. But I promise you that we will visit the Bishop soon."

Three months later, Lucy returned from India to Dar es Salaam and stopped in to see Enekia and other old friends. Enekia said that, since Lucy was in Dar, they should go see Bishop Eliudi. Lucy had heard about the School of Evangelism in Sakila. In fact, one of her Assembly of God pastors had attended the school. As a result, she had a desired to see the school. But Lucy had been away from her business for three months and felt that she could not be absent any longer. However, Enekia told Lucy that she had promised Bishop Eliudi that she and Lucy would come to see him. After a little more discussion, Lucy said that she would go for a quick visit of two days only.

The two women traveled to Sakila and stayed for two nights in Bishop Eliudi's guest rooms. Lucy liked the rural area around Sakila and had a desire to someday to live in a village like Sakila where she could grow fresh vegetables. On their last breakfast there, Bishop came to talk with Lucy. Mama Lucy told Bishop that if God ever led him to Mozambique, he should stop and see her. She pointed out that both of them loved serving God. They exchanged business cards before Lucy went back to Dar es Salaam with Enekia.

In Dar es Salaam, Lucy learned that a three day Morris Cerullo crusade was going to be held in that city. She decided to stay on with Enekia just a few more days to attend the crusade. From Dar, Lucy emailed Eliudi to thank him for his hospitality. Two days later Eliudi emailed her back and asked her where she was. Lucy replied that she was still in Dar waiting for the Cerullo crusade to begin. Eliudi then mentioned that he would be in Dar to attend that crusade as well. Maybe they could meet at that time. Lucy replied that a get-together would be acceptable to her. Mama Lucy at this point had no feelings for Eliudi other than that for a Christian brother.

When Bishop Eliudi arrived in Dar es Salaam, he was invited to breakfast with Morris Cerullo. He called Enekia and asked if she and Lucy would like to go to the breakfast with him. After that breakfast was over, Bishop Eliudi wanted to talk privately with the gregarious Lucy. He asked her if she liked being a widow and wanted to live that way for the rest of her life. Or, could she consider another romance in her life? Lucy laughed nervously over those questions. She replied that she may not be ready for the ups and downs of marriage again. However, if God brought a Christian man into her life, she might reconsider her future. Eliudi leaned closer to Lucy and said, "If that be the case, I think that here I am."

Lucy replied, "Maybe that is so. Let us leave it in the hands of God for the time being." The two prayed together and parted. Lucy went back to Mozambique with the understanding that if God wanted them together, He would make it happen. Meanwhile, Eliudi was off on one of his trips to America.

Bishop Eliudi would frequently call Lucy. While in America, he would use his cell phone to call in the morning and in the evening just to talk to her. She would lock herself in her bedroom to talk to him for hours on end. Lucy's oldest son would question her and ask her what she was doing in her bedroom. He would say, "Mama, what is going on with you? I hear you giggling a lot." However, Lucy kept the conversations with Eliudi to herself.

Late in 2010 Eliudi talked to Godwin about his blossoming romance with Lucy. As the oldest son, Godwin could stop the relationship at any time and Eliudi would have to respect that decision. Since Helen had administered every detail of their domestic life, Godwin saw how difficult it had been for Eliudi without Helen helping him manage the home and the family farm. Godwin happily gave his consent to his father to continue to court Lucy and left any other major decisions entirely up to him.

One day Lucy told Bishop about the man's shirt that had been hanging in her closet for many years. She told Eliudi that if he tried the shirt on and it fit with him liking it, then she would know that their romance was from God.

On one of her visits to her family in Dar es Salaam, Lucy left the shirt with

Enekia for Bishop to try on the next time he was in town. Later, she got a telephone call from Eliudi that he had put on her shirt, it fit wonderfully and he loved the color. He felt that it was time for them to get married. With that, Lucy accepted the proposal.

Even though both Eliudi and Lucy had been married before, a dowry was still needed from Eliudi to Lucy's family to officially condone the marriage. Lucy's family was from a different tribe than Eliudi and did not require large dowries. At the most they gave money, some chickens and maybe a goat. On the other hand, the Meru tribe believed in giving larger dowries. There was a clear difference of what was to be expected as a dowry for Lucy. Since Eliudi was a Bishop, Lucy's family indicated that they would just let him decide on what to give. He eventually gave a cow and four sheep to Lucy's mother and uncle. (Lucy's father had died some years before and her uncle was acting as the head of the family.)

Eliudi and Lucy were married in July of 2011 at the church in Sakila.

Now it is time to think about the future of the International Evangelism Church in central Africa. One thing that Eliudi and his staff are praying for is that the economy improves worldwide which will free up some much needed funds for projects that are on hold. Moses Mafie, the lead teacher at the evangelism school, also adds that he would like to have two busses that could be used to transport school students to markets and local cities where they could evangelize.

Currently a new church building is being constructed in Sakila. This building will be located outside the IEC school campus and in the local community. It is hoped that more people will attend the services in the new church as they will not have to enter the walled campus. At this point, the foundation for the new church has been laid. The existing church building will continue to be a conference hall for the School of Evangelism.

As the reader will see later in this book, a new health clinic is nearing completion. That facility is also located across the main road from the school's campus.

In Arusha more buildings are about to be constructed at the orphanage.

The first orphan house was just competed in 2014. The house holds ten of the older orphaned girls, giving them more privacy than living in the current dormitory rooms. When funding comes available, a second orphan house will be built for the ten oldest boys. The long range plan is to build more houses so that eventually there will be 200 children at the orphanage.

Currently Bishop Eliudi is broadcasting a weekly half hour program from a local radio station. However, IEC is in the process of building a radio station in Arusha for full time Christian broadcasts. This came about in 2009 when a Tanzanian lady asked Eliudi if he wanted to purchase a hilltop located just north of the orphanage. She felt that she had to sell the land specifically to the IEC church. At that time Bishop Eliudi said that he was not interested in buying the land. The lady left but returned a week later to have Eliudi reconsider her offer. Again Eliudi said that he did not have a need for the land. The lady was at least persistent, if nothing else, for a few weeks later she again returned and wanted Eliudi to go with her to look at the hill. Eliudi agreed to at least view the property from the crest of its hill. While there and looking out over the city, he felt inspired to reach out to all the people in the city and the surrounding countryside. The land was purchased and the location for a new radio station was established.

While in America in February of 2011, Bishop Eliudi met the general manager of Your Network of Praise (YNOP) Radio, Roger Lonnequist of Helena, MT. Eliudi explained his vision of a radio transmitter to Roger and told him about the hill that he had purchased. Eliudi was calling the proposed station the New Life Radio. Roger had been working toward expanding his network internationally and the idea of a radio station in Tanzania appealed to him.

On November 21, 2011, a blessing came by the way of YNOP Radio. They held a fund raiser on the air for the Tanzanian station project. In just one hour, $10,000 was raised for the New Life Radio project in Arusha. With the help of that donation, a three room building was constructed on the top of the hill. Transmitting equipment will now need to be secured for the building. Personnel will need to be hired and trained to operate the radio station and to plan its programming. Progress is being made in Arusha to put the radio station on the air.

And that was how Eliudi's vision progressed and has overcome many obstacles. But this is not the end of Bishop Eliudi's amazing story. In the following chapters you will read in deeper detail how these inspired projects developed and how more people have become thoroughly involved to reflect Eliudi's vision. There are many God ordained miracles still waiting to be told.

Bishop Eliudi Issangya stands at the "bell" that is used to waken and summon the School of Evangelism students to morning prayer meetings. This 2012 photograph shows the men's dormitory directly behind Eliudi.
D. Simmering photograph

Eliudi and Helen Issangya are seen in years after the evangelism school was established and flourishing.
IEO Photograph Collection – J. Kinley

From early 2013, a class of men and women ministry students is ready to start a new session of study in Sakila. The course will continue for six months.
IEO Photograph Collection

Trusty Matheson's well drilling rig is set up and working to bring potable water to the people of Tanzania. This village was one of the many towns where wells were established in 2009.
T. Matheson Photograph

These smiling children were part of the very first class of elementary students at the Sluys/Anderson school in 2003.

G. Anderson Photograph

The Crower Trade School students learn numerous skills that will support them in life. In this photograph, the students are using their training to construct a church building with cement blocks.

IEO Photograph Collection

The orphans of Christ Hope Orphanage in Arusha, TZ are dressed in their public school uniforms and ready for a day of learning.
IEO Photograph Collection

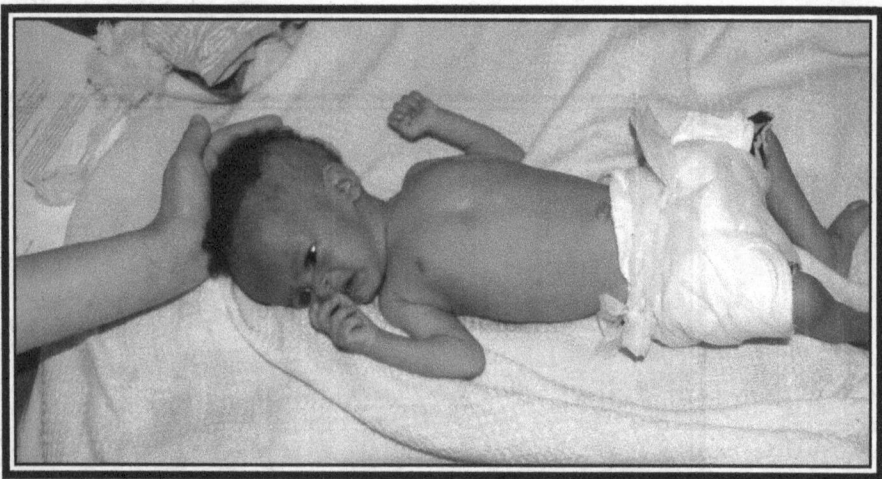

Baby Claire was brought to Sakila Clinic in May 2011. She was near starvation as her mother's breast milk had dried up. To keep the baby alive, the mother was feeding the child cow's milk. See chapter 19 for Baby Claire's story.
B. Miller Photograph

This is the front of the conference hall/church that Eliudi Issangya built in Sakila between 1992 and 1996.

D. Simmering Photograph

Bishop Eliudi has had two faithful supporters over the years of his IEC ministry. They are Moses Mafie (L) and John Matthew (R) who are pictured at a relaxed outdoor meeting typical of the African culture.

D. Simmering Photograph

A new health clinic is under construction in Sakila, TZ. A portion of the building is seen as it was in 2012. The new clinic will greatly expand the room available to treat sick and injured patients.

D. Simmering Photograph

A goat is being roasted over an open fire before it is served at a feast in Tanzania.

T. Matheson Photograph

The first informal children's school in Sakila was held in a converted chicken coup. Pictured are the children of that pre-school of 1998. From this humble beginning, the Sluys/Anderson primary school and the Sakila Hebron Secondary School came into existence.

G. Anderson Photograph

After the death of his first wife, Eliudi married Lucy in July of 2011. This photograph was taken on the day of their wedding.

M. Sluys Photograph

PART 2:
Reflecting The Vision

CHAPTER 7:

GO INTO ALL THE WORLD
(Mark 16:15)

While in California in January of 1983, Eliudi Issangya attended the annual Morris Cerullo Conference. As he was milling around the lecture hall at the conference, he met a lady by the name of Grace Bedsole and struck up a conversation with her. After talking to him for a short time, she invited Eliudi to join her group. At the table were her son Jim Bedsole and his wife Shirley. (Jim is the pastor at the First Assembly of God Church in El Cajon.) Also seated at the table were their friends, Bruce and Barbara Crower.

After everyone was acquainted, Eliudi wasted no time in telling them about his School of Evangelism. He shared several photographs of the buildings which he had constructed in Sakila. (At that time, photographs were expensive and hard to obtain in Tanzania.) Before the night was over, Jim and Shirley invited Eliudi to stay at their home while he was in the area. He accepted their offer and was with the Bedsoles for the next three weeks.

The Bedsoles saw the vision of Eliudi's heart and his desire to further the work of God through his school. Since Jim and Shirley were convinced of the validity of Eliudi's mission, they introduced him to other churches in the area during those three weeks.

Before Eliudi left the Bedsole's home, he asked them to come and teach at the newly-built School of Evangelism in Sakila. He removed a calendar from the wall and looked for dates during which Jim and Shirley could help instruct the first enrolled class. Since Jim was a new pastor with three children, he did not have a lot of disposable money on hand. In 1983 the flight to Africa would cost Jim and Shirley around $2,000. That was money that they did not have. For them $2,000 in airfare might as well be two million dollars.

In true Eliudi fashion, he said that the cost of getting there was not important. He explained, "God will provide the funding. What we are going to do now is lay our hands on the calendar and pray for this trip to happen. I want you to come to Tanzania for five weeks and help with the first class of students." Jim and Shirley put their faith in God and said that they would be there even though they did not know how their travel expenses would be paid.

That evening, Eliudi went to the Crower's home for dinner. Bruce showed Eliudi his home and photographs of his Indianapolis-style race car and personal airplane. During dinner Eliudi again shared his vision of the school in Sakila with Bruce and Barbara. Then he told them, "Pastor Jim and Shirley are planning to come to Tanzania to teach. You should come with them." During that designated time Bruce and Barbara had planned on going on a tour of Israel. After some thought, Bruce decided to cancel his Israel trip and agreed to visit Sakila. Near the close of the evening, Bruce added, "Tell Jim and Shirley that since they are going over to Tanzania, we will go with them and I will cover the cost of their airline tickets."

Before Eliudi left the Crower's home, he indicated that one of the pressing needs at the school was a local supply of clean water. He explained that the people in his village had to walk four miles to collect water from a river and haul it back in containers strapped to the backs of donkeys, placed in a wheel barrow or balanced on the top of their heads. "We need a water source on the campus," Eliudi explained. Bruce, as it happened, was a very mechanically inclined individual. Within a few days he began to research how he could help alleviate the unhealthy and limited water conditions in Sakila. Bruce was certain that he could devise a solution to mediate their water situation.

Eliudi was very pleased with the way things were turning out. He had had a number of disappointments during his time in California, but his contacts were starting to bear fruit.

While Bruce and Barbara were getting equipment together to drill water wells, the Bedsoles were also busy. Jim was collecting teaching materials for use at the African school. Since Shirley is gifted musically, she visited music stores asking for donations of guitars and guitar strings for the Tanzanian ministry. She also gathered sheet music of worship songs to have translated into Swahili once they arrived in Sakila.

What they took with them to Africa, they would have to hand-carry on the airplane or check-in as luggage. The only items sent on ahead to Tanzania were the well drilling machine and some hand pumps that Bruce had designed and assembled. Those objects were shipped by air freight to Sakila to be sure that that they would be there when the El Cajon visitors arrived. Luckily the drilling machine that Bruce designed and built was compact.

Not knowing what to expect when they arrived in Sakila, the Bedsoles and the Crowers left for Tanzania with high expectations. After a series of long flights, the group landed at the Kilimanjaro Airport. The terminal at that time was simply a cement-block building with a roof and no conveniences for travelers. There was no place to buy a meal or get a drink of water. There was no toilet paper in the restrooms - no frills. However, the group was amazed at being greeted by a crowd of people from Sakila who were waving at them from the observation platform.

When Tanzanian customs at the airport inspected their belongings, they just dumped everything out of their bags and examined each item one piece at a time. Soldiers with automatic weapons were guarding the structure and the surrounding area. The visitors felt a bit intimidated by all of this and wondered what they had gotten themselves into. After clearing customs, Eliudi was there to greet them along with the delegation from the school. One smiling lady in the crowd was Eliudi's wife, Helen. This was the Americans' first time to meet her. She was to hold a very special place in their hearts in the years to come.

The visitors loaded their gear and baggage into Eliudi's Land Rover and a truck. Departing the airport, they traveled into the countryside. Within the first few miles of leaving the airport, they discovered that the condition of the roads in Tanzania left a lot to be desired. Turning off the main road, it was still a 20 minute ride to Sakila even though the distance was only four kilometers. The deep ruts in the steep, dirt road were frightening.

When they arrived at the campus in Sakila, they saw the four school buildings that Eliudi had told them about. Even though there was almost no landscaping and absolutely no security fencing, the buildings were more than adequate. Eliudi showed the Bedsoles and Crowers where they were to stay. They were provided beds in a building where the school teachers normally slept. The Westerners made themselves at home and were excited to finally be in Tanzania.

After a few days, the group found out that drinking water was indeed a major problem at the campus. The Californians had not brought water purifying pills with them and at that time there was no bottled water in Tanzania available to purchase. At the school, everyone drank either water hauled from the river or rain water that had run off of the roofs and collected in fifty-five gallon oil drums. The water that the Californians drank from the drums was light brown, the color of weak tea. When the people of the village drank the water, it did not seem to adversely affect them.

However, the Bedsoles and Crowers all came down with what they called "Tanzania Revenge." Shirley was the first to become sick from the water. She was rapidly followed by the rest of the group. They became so ill that Bruce was ready to send for Paul Toma, a doctor from their church. Even though the doctor was never contacted, Bruce thought that Dr. Toma could be flown to Tanzania to help them overcome the "revenge." Everyone, including Eliudi, was concerned about the group's physical condition.

While Barbara and Shirley were "helping" in the kitchen, they watched the local ladies as they were washing the dishes. The plates were cleaned with lye soap and scrubbed with corn husks. The dishes were not rinsed after washing but simply left in the sun to dry. Barbara and Shirley believed that the harmful lye residue that was left on the eating utensils was being ingested with their food. They also noticed that the kitchen ladies were cooking with unrefrigerated goat fat and not the purified cooking oil that the Westerners were accustomed to.

Eliudi continued to watch the physical condition of his guests and knew that he had to make some changes. A plan was agreed upon that only simple cooked rice and beans were what the group would eat during their visit. Even with all the illnesses and cultural adjusting, the hearts of the missionaries were enamored with the warmth of the people in Sakila.

To help with communications, the Bedsoles and the Crowers tried to learn Swahili. However, there were only three people at the school who could speak English. As a result, communication and progress was slow. Barbara and Shirley spent hours with Helen while she cooked. During those sessions with Helen, they learned Swahili words for certain items, got to know the people and tried to comprehend African customs.

There were twenty students in the first class and none of them were able to speak English. Pastor Jim was leading classes every day with all the teaching being accomplished through a translator. Shirley also instructed several of the sessions. She sang and taught a few of the songs that had been translated. These efforts were the beginning of Jim and Shirley's struggle to learn Swahili.

One day a few weeks into their stay, Jim taught on the gifts of the Holy Spirit. After he finished teaching, he asked for an altar call for anyone wanting to receive those gifts. Jim and Shirley laid hands on the students that came forward and prayed for them. The students would then start speaking in tongues but what they were saying was unknown to Jim and Shirley. To them all of their spoken words sounded like Swahili or some other mysterious language. As always, Eliudi was with the Bedsoles teaching and watching the outpouring of the Spirit. Jim had to ask Eliudi if the students were speaking in tongues. Eliudi confirmed to them that was indeed what was taking place.

However, one student was heard exclaiming, "Blessed be the Lord our God Almighty!" and speaking other phrases in perfect English. Jim and Shirley looked at each other and wondered if possibly he had previously known English. They asked Eliudi about the individual to which he replied, "This man is from the African bush. How could he know English? He has never spoken English before in his life!" Jim and Shirley were astonished at the miraculous outpouring and had their own faith strengthen by the manifestations of the Spirit. At the time, Jim Bedsole was 30 years of age and had never seen anything like it during his ministry in the United States.

While the Bedsoles were working at the school in 1983, a water baptism was planned for a few new believers. Bishop Eliudi asked if Jim would baptize his oldest son, Godwin, who was 13 years old at the time. Of course Jim willingly agreed to that. The only body of water deep enough to baptize anyone in the village was a swampy area north of the school. Although Jim was excited about the baptism, he was apprehensive about what would be lurking in the murky swamp water. Through his contacts, Jim had confirmed the presence of blood-sucking leaches in the muddy mire. On the day of the baptism, Jim put on a pair of long pants and tucked the leg material into his socks. He also wrapped cloth around his shoes and ankles to help keep the leaches away from his skin.

After Godwin's baptism ceremony, others who were being baptized gave their testimony of how God had and was blessing their lives. A local woman told how she had been afflicted with demons and how God had healed her. She was crying and praising God as she was baptized. Jim explains,

"When God heals in the wildernesses of Africa, He really heals." Jim and Shirley were inspired by the people's faith. Africa was raw and primitive, but the people had a genuine desire to know God. God's holiness was working mightily in their lives.

One of the regular away-from-the-village excursions that Eliudi took the Bedsoles on was a drive to the airport to pick up the mail. This trip always occurred on Thursdays as the only plane to land at the Kilimanjaro Airport at the time was on Thursday. If passengers arrived at Kilimanjaro, it was Thursday. If someone wanted to leave Tanzania and missed the Thursday airplane, they waited until the following Thursday to catch the next one. Even though the plane was supposed to arrive at a certain time, it could also arrive hours late. (With the growing popularity of wild animal safaris and mountain climbing treks in Tanzania, the complexion of the Kilimanjaro Airport has changed, including better amenities and more frequent flights.)

Shirley loved to take photographs with her camera. Of course, the people of northern Tanzania and southern Kenya were quite picturesque. When driving to or from the airport, she would try to take photographs of the Masai. However, that tribe did not want their image captured on film. In order to get the desired photographs of the Masai, she had to become very discrete with her camera.

On Sundays Bruce and Barbara Crower would give greetings to the church in Sakila. They would also include testimonies of God's guidance in their lives. Shirley would sing and Jim would preach to the people of the village.

One Sunday a local man showed up and sat secretly at the back of the church. This man was a witchdoctor and had arrived to put a curse on the Bedsoles' and Crowers' ministry. This witchdoctor was a rich man and owned many goats. He would charge the locals large sums of money to use his goats in witchcraft rites and sacrifices which he conducted. This shaman held enormous power over many of people living in the surrounding area.

Jim's Sunday message that day was that Jesus is coming again. The evangelism school students performed a drama about the end times. Some of the student actors on the stage were boasting, "We are eating well and very happy. We do not need Jesus." While another group of actors were warning, "Repent and get ready! Jesus is coming back to take his followers with him to Heaven." Then a student entered onto the stage dressed as the grim reaper - death. The actors who denied needing Jesus were taken away uttering tormented moaning and crying. Next an actor dressed as Jesus came on the stage to save his faithful people. There were many happy faces and much rejoicing from those actors.

After the play and a sermon, an altar call was given to the congregation to receive salvation. The witch doctor was the first person to stand up and run from the back of the church to the stage. He went straight to Jim and demanded that Jim immediately lay his hands on him as he wanted to receive God's redemption. He desperately cried that he wanted to go to Heaven when he died - to be with Jesus.

Later the ex-witchdoctor explained that during the play he had actually seen Satan coming towards him to take him to Hell. It was an aberration that only the shaman saw as no one else in the church had noticed anything out of the ordinary. The local people who knew the individual were amazed at his conversion as that man had made a profitable living from his witchcraft practices. When he accepted salvation in Jesus he rejected that past life. Jim says to this day that it was a great victory that Sunday for Jesus.

Also that year Pastor Jim encouraged Eliudi to consider admitting women to the school in order that they could study for the ministry. Including women in what was considered a man's domain was not the "norm" for the culture of Tanzania. However Eliudi understood that the call of active faith was for women as well as men. By 1986, Eliudi had enrolled the first three women at the School of Evangelism.

Meanwhile, Bruce Crower had set up his well drilling machine and was working ten hours a day to bring clean water to the village. Those were long hard days with many challenges. Fortunately, he had a number of local men helping with the task. The men that helped Bruce were personally selected by Eliudi for their demonstrated mechanical abilities. However, Bruce did not know how to speak Swahili. As a result Bruce had written on the palm of his hand a few phrases of Swahili that he could use to instruct his helpers. Among the phrases he used were: *What is your name; Turn to*

the right; Turn to the left; and *Stand back.*

Another well drilling challenge was having something as straightforward as having two pieces of pipe welded together. To accomplish that simple task, it took most of Bruce's day to drive into Arusha with the pipe and complete a search to locate a competent welder.

From all of Bruce's efforts, five wells were drilled. The maximum depth that the drilling machine would penetrate into the ground was 200 feet, but that was a sufficient depth to hit water at the school in Sakila. When the hand pumps were installed, clean water flowed into the village for the very first time. These wells continued to pump water for many years. One by one they eventually filled with sediment and ceased to produce. A more permanent solution would have to be found later. But in 1983, the clean water was a huge blessing.

Bruce not only drilled the wells, he also tried to teach the members of the village how to use the drilling equipment. When he returned to the States, he left the well drilling machinery and the blessings of clean water in Sakila.

Bruce and Barbara's developing concern was that the men and women of the village did not have the skills that they required to progress to the next level of self-sufficiency. Bruce approached Eliudi with the idea of starting a trade school for anyone who did not want to become a pastor, but who needed a marketable talent. After the discussion, land was purchased between Kikatiti and Arusha where Eliudi had a new building constructed. Eliudi named the building the Crower Trade School. The students would eventually be able to learn masonry, carpentry, welding, sewing and home economics. The students at the trade school were charged $30 a year for the training.

CHAPTER 8:

PROCLAIM THE ETERNAL GOSPEL

(Rev 14:6)

In 1986, the Bedsoles returned for another visit to Sakila. This time they brought a musical keyboard with them so that Shirley could start an instrumental music class. Some of the students from that first class are still playing their instruments for current church services. Whatever the individual African's level of music ability became, they always had fun making music.

Jim and Shirley also transported a TV, a video cassette player and a number of teaching video tapes with them on the trip. They hosted movie nights in the village and made popcorn for those in attendance. (At the time, a portable generator supplied the electricity.) One of the tapes that they brought along was the Ten Commandments starring Charlton Heston. Of course, the movie was in English, so a translation was provided when it was shown.

For the showing of the Ten Commandments the room was packed with people around the little TV screen. During the scene where Moses defended Jethro's daughters from the men who were stealing the girls' water at the well, the audience cheered for Moses. When the Pharaoh's daughter was seducing Moses, the people understood right away what was being portrayed on the screen. As the TV showed her lying on the coach luring Moses, the men shouted out "hapana! (no!)" Meanwhile, the women hid their eyes during that scene and moaned that they knew what she was planning to do. When Moses was in shackles, a symphony of crying cascaded from the audience for Moses. Hollywood productions were all new to the villagers and they were amazed at what they saw. However, the God-centered messages of the video tapes were inspiring the local people. Popcorn and miracles do go together, at least in rural Africa.

Eliudi had found some pedal-driven sewing machines to place in the Crower Trade School and asked Shirley to teach the women how to sew clothes with the machines. The first difficulty that she had was instructing the women to correctly pump the treadles on the sewing machines with their feet. For some reason, it was difficult for the women to master the motions. Eventually Shirley had to place the girls feet on the treadles and move their feet with her hands. The women would break out in laughter at having someone touch their feet. Every time she touched their feet, they would fall off of their chairs and roll on the floor laughing. Shirley would try to contain their laughter by saying "focus girls!" That admonition was of no use, for even the translator was laughing.

Soon after the first class graduated from the Bible School, Eliudi took his cue from the Cerullo School of Ministry that he had attended in San Diego and planned yearly conferences for the graduates to reunite in Sakila. Jim and Shirley often traveled back to Sakila to attend those annual conferences. There would frequently be thousands of people in attendance at these sessions. Since the conference hall at that time was too small for such a large number of people, the meetings were held outside.

One day after a reunion conference, Jim and Shirley were walking down the road from Sakila when a young man driving a tractor stopped beside them. He said in very good English, "Hello, I remember you. I recall the first conference that you conducted outdoors. I had to sit way in the back, out beside the road to listen to you preach. Ever since then I have been living for Jesus." Jim exclaimed, "Great! That is what I have been waiting to hear." Jim and Shirley were all smiles at the young man's testimony.

Not all of the Bedsole's time with Eliudi was allotted to preaching and teaching. When they prepared to go to Africa in 2008 with 12 other members from their El Cajon church, the First Assembly of God, they planned to accomplish a makeover of the school. They went with a mission to repaint all of the school classrooms and the trim on the buildings plus tile the bathrooms and office space. To complete these tasks they had sent ahead 150 gallons of paint, numerous pallets of tile along with grout and all the necessary tools.

In 2010 the Bedsoles went back to Sakila for Rocky's, Eliudi's son, wedding and to once again teach at the School of Evangelism. The class at that time numbered 100 students, both male and female. Once more teaching on the gifts of the Spirit, Jim asked for an altar call when 30 students came forward. One of the students was unable to walk to the front because she had a horrible fever. Before her friends got her up and carried her to the class, that sick student had been confined to her bed during the previous few days. Moses Mafie, a leader at the Bible School, informed Shirley that the girl was very ill and needed special prayer.

The students helped the sick girl to the front of the gathering, as she could not stand on her own. Shirley and Moses laid their hands on her feverish skin. Shirley, who had placed her hand on the girl's forehead, said, "In the Name of Jesus, we come against this sickness. Fever, you have to be gone in Jesus' name." Moses, who had his hand on the girl's back, looked up at Shirley startled and exclaimed, "Did you feel that?" Both Shirley and Moses had felt the sick girl's fever break as her skin instantly cooled to normal. Even the student was amazed at how she had become well so suddenly. Everyone in attendance at the meeting was excited about that answer to prayer. When the meeting was over, the healed girl met her friends who wanted to help her back to her bed. Instead she countered, "No, I am healed. My fever is gone!" In fact she felt so well that she went out and gathered wood for the evening cooking fires.

During the October 2010 School of Evangelism session, northern Tanzania was in disparate need of rain. The people who live around Sakila are farmers and grow crops for a living. They depend on the rain to make those crops grow and mature. When the rains do not come at the appointed time, the plants die and the people go hungry. Because of this, everyone was earnestly praying and fasting for rain.

After a chapel prayer meeting, the Bedsoles went back to their room to rest. While relaxing, Shirley was trying to remember a Swahili word that she wanted to use. As she looked in her Swahili dictionary, she found the word that she sought. As she read the definition of that word, she noticed the next word just below that one had a definition meaning "it will rain." Shirley exclaimed to Jim, "My Swahili dictionary says it is going to rain! And do you know what; I believe that it is going to rain before we leave for home. I believe that in my heart. I am going to tell the school staff that God is going to send rain soon."

Excitedly she ran to the school staff and told them in Swahili that it was going to rain before she and Jim would leave for America. Many people heard her tell the school leaders this good news. On the fringe of the crowd was the night watchman of the school. Even though the sky was crystal clear with not a cloud in sight, he had tucked his pant legs into his socks and had his umbrella up and deployed. Shirley looked quizzically at the night watchman and asked the staff, "What is he doing?" A teacher at the school replied, "He has heard you say that you believe that it is going to rain. He is simply getting prepared for it to happen at any time." However, it did not rain that day.

For the next two days people at the school campus met each other exclaiming, "I believe that it is going to rain!" Jim and Shirley fervently prayed for that rain. They needed a miracle rain to not only water the crops but to increase the faith of the village. On the second night, Jim and Shirley went out in the dark and looked up at the immense African sky, filled with twinkling stars. They saw one little cloud on a distant horizon. Shirley pointed at the cloud and confidently told Jim, "That is the cloud that will bring the rain."

The next morning there was heard a steady drumming on the tin roof. Soon happy people were banging on their door. After months without even a drizzle, rain clouds were wetting the dusty ground. The people of the village were so excited, "Look Mama, it is raining! It is a miracle." The rain was the gentle, life-giving rain that the crops needed to grow.

The day after the rainfall was Rocky's wedding. The rain stopped long enough to have a clear, cloudless sky for the wedding. After the wedding, Jim and Shirley took a walk down the hill from Sakila. The weather was hot and humid as they hiked. A short way down the road, the wind picked up and a storm cloud gathered on the horizon. They looked at each other and decided it was time to quickly stride back to Sakila.

No sooner had they found shelter under the eve of a building when the rain fell again. People from across the campus commons shouted to them, "It is raining! It is a miracle! You have taught us faith." Shirley turned to Jim and said, "Today, God has taught me faith!" After the rain showers, one of the students said, "We are all sons of Abraham." His faith had also been encouraged. After the Bedsoles returned home to San Diego, they received a message from Eliudi saying that it was still raining in Sakila.

The latest project Jim and Shirley's church has undertaken is the shipping of mountain bikes to Sakila. Newly ordained pastors need a way to move around in Africa. Since fuel and automobiles are so expensive in Tanzania, a bicycle is a viable way to travel from town to town. In earlier years, Americans donated second-hand bikes which were collected and shipped to the school. However, some of the bikes were so used that they were beyond repair. Other bikes collected had the narrower racing tires which could not be used on the dirt trails in Africa.

Finally, Eliudi requested that the Bedsoles take up a collection and buy new mountain bikes for the graduating pastors. During the first year of the project, their church sent over 17 new bikes and they felt excited about what they had accomplished. However, they kept on praying for the bike program. The following year they were able to purchase 26 bicycles for the pastors graduating from the school. In 2011, the church was able to purchase 60 bikes. Then in 2012, a total of 91 new mountain bikes was sent to the School of Evangelism.

The Bedsoles have supported other portions of Eliudi's ministry in Tanzania and in other countries as well. But they are pastors and their hearts are with the school in Sakila. They continue to focus on that segment of the mission, insuring that the Gospel is preached around the world.

Jim says, "I have heard it said that some ministries can grow thirty, sixty, one hundred fold as God blesses them. However, I have never seen a ministry grow hundred fold; that is until I observed the things that Eliudi has accomplished in the past 30 years. His work has been blessed by God a hundred fold."

CHAPTER 9:
HEAL THOSE WHO NEED HEALING
(Luke 9:11)

A person would think that a medical mission in Sakila would have been a top priority for Bishop Eliudi. But with Eliudi focused mainly on the School of Evangelism, it took a few years before the medical work in Sakila started to flourish. The path to establish a medical clinic there took a number of interesting twists and turns. This narrative starts on another one of Eliudi's tours to visit his supporting churches in the United States.

The story begins in rural Stayton, Oregon. Jan George is a nurse who became a Christian in 1973. After she was converted, she felt that she was being strongly drawn to foreign mission fields in order to medically help less fortunate people. Since her husband, Roger, was not a Christian at the time, her dream of overseas mission trips was put on hold. Roger did become a Christian later in 1974 and as a family they began to attend a local church.

Years later, the Georges attended a home fellowship. During that time they provided a home for some exchange students and foster kids. One of the foster girls who was living with the Georges had a bad accident and fractured her hip in four or five different places. Jan called the girl's mother and explained what had happened. Even though the injured girl's mother lived in Montana, she gladly volunteered to come to Stayton to help nurse her daughter back to health.

While the injured girl's mother was staying in Stayton, she mentioned that she knew a couple from Tanzania who were doing some wonderful work there. That couple had connections in Montana, California and Washington State and would love to find someone to support them from Oregon.

Roger and Jan thought it over and prayed about this couple. Finally they went to their fellowship members and asked if they should invite the couple from Tanzania to speak at their gathering. There was a consensus that a guest speaker would be welcomed. On January 5, 1987, Eliudi and Helen Issangya came to visit Roger and Jan at their rural home. They were driven by car from California to meet the Oregonians with whom they would stay for a week. Roger and Jan fell in love with Eliudi and his wife, Helen, right away and decided to help them as much as possible. Of course, Eliudi was always looking for assistance for his evangelism school.

On a Friday night and in separate cars, Jan drove Helen and Roger drove Eliudi to Salem to speak at a Youth With A Mission (YWAM) gathering. Keep in mind, Roger and Jan always talk over and weigh major decisions together before committing or rejecting them. On the way home from the YWAM base, Helen mentioned to Jan that her oldest son, Godwin, needed to come to America to get a good education. She explained that the schools in Tanzania were at best poorly taught. She wondered if Jan would consent to having Godwin stay at her house so that he could attend the local public high school. The Georges had four children (two boys and two girls) of their own at home at the time. Since Roger and Jan also had foster kids and foreign exchange students occasionally residing at their house, Jan felt that they could definitely consider Helen's request. Meanwhile, Eliudi was asking Roger the same question in his car. Roger said that he might be agreeable to Eliudi's request. Both Roger and Jan had independently said "yes, maybe" to the educating of Eliudi's oldest son without discussing it with the other spouse.

When Roger and Jan got home, they compared their independent decisions about Godwin and were happy to find that they were in mutual agreement. Before they left Oregon, Eliudi and Helen said that there were other families who were considering housing Godwin to insure that he got a good education. Eliudi indicated that perhaps he would later contact the Georges about them hosting Godwin.

In March, Eliudi called the Georges and told them that Helen and he had decided to send Godwin to them. The reality of having another son in the family began to sink in. In August, Eliudi called from Africa to say that Godwin would soon be on his way to Oregon.

At the appointed arrival time, Roger, Jan, their youngest daughter and a Japanese exchange student went to the airport in Portland to pick up Godwin. When Godwin got off of the plane they immediately knew who he was. In a sea of casually dressed passengers, there was a young man by himself and who looked lost. He was dressed in a suit and had the George's name and telephone number written on the palm of his hand. That information must have been written there before he had departed Sakila. He carried no photographs of the family that he was to meet to help identify them. All that Godwin knew concerning his sponsors was inked on his hand.

Before leaving for the United States, Godwin had never been more than 30 miles away from his home. Since Sakila was a remote village located in the foothills of Mt. Kilimanjaro, very few visitors passed through his home village. Now he was in a bustling country where everything moved much faster than he was used to. To complicate this situation, the Georges were surprised to learn that Godwin spoke very little English.

When Jan called Eliudi, she informed him that his son had arrived safely at their home. Eliudi corrected her and said, "He is no longer just my son. He is your son as well." This was no student exchange program; Jan suddenly realized that this was a long term situation. Jan also thought, "How can Eliudi and Helen send their oldest son to live half way around the world to a home where they had only spent a week? They must love Godwin very much and trust that God's will would be done for him."

The day after Godwin arrived, Kelly (the George's youngest son) and one of his friends drove Godwin to Salem and introduced him to Winchell's Doughnuts and Toys-R-Us. Godwin was totally amazed at what he saw and experienced.

Even with all the new experiences, Godwin suffered from home sickness while lying in his American bed at night. The room where Godwin stayed had basketball players printed on the wall paper. Godwin later said that he would lie in bed, look at those strange figures on the wall and wonder what those men were doing.

One of the first things for Jan to accomplish was to register Godwin as a junior at the local high school. At this point, their problems really began. The visa that allowed Godwin to come to America was not the normal educational visa that he required to attend school in the United States. However after a lot of explaining by the Georges, the public school enrolled Godwin on that visa.

After going through Godwin's suitcase, Jan realized that he had very few clothes or shoes for school. She took him shopping and had fun watching his eyes light up with each new purchase. Jan then drove Godwin, who was wearing his new clothes, to the local high school to sign him up for his classes. It was during this process that Roger and Jan realized that Godwin was another child in their family to be raised, loved, taught, encouraged and disciplined. They were responsible to take care of all his needs and mentor him through high school.

Godwin was a quick learner and was able to master the English language in about three months. Plus, he learned the necessary American slang words in quick order. It seemed that Godwin felt that the sooner he stopped speaking Swahili, the better off he would be.

While he attended classes, Godwin wanted to enter sports, drama and music activities conducted after school. However, that was not easily accomplished as the school administration felt that they could not let Godwin participate in extra-curricular activities. Jan discovered that Godwin's legal status was again causing the problem. The administrators at the school were concerned about who had the authorized responsibility for Godwin's safety and actions during those after-school events.

Ultimately, it was determined that the Georges would have to become Godwin's legal guardians to eliminate problems with the visa status. This new status gave him all of the opportunities that children of tax payers are entitled to. The Georges also had to enroll him on their medical insurance. After all this was accomplished, Jan wrote letters to the high school asking permission for Godwin to participate in any chosen functions during and after school. That permission was granted. Once these requests were approved, most of the high school legal difficulties concerning Godwin were eliminated.

In high school, Godwin played football, went out for track and was selected for an elite singing group along with his Oregon brother and sister. He also acquired his driver's license and shared a car with the other kids in the family. However, Godwin was disappointed that the school had no soccer team that he could join.

The Georges owned a two-story home which was surrounded by many large farms. During the summer, Godwin and his two brothers worked on the neighboring farms to earn money for school expenses, car outlays and spending money. The boys learned the value of hard work and on some days got home late in the evening after bailing hay or harvesting grain for market.

During his subsequent tours of the United States each year, Eliudi would visit the George's home and become re-acquainted with his son. Not only did the Georges now have five children (including Godwin), but the children also had two fathers. While Eliudi was in Roger's home, he was father to all of the children as well. He grew very close to Roger and Jan's children as they accepted him as an additional father. Eliudi was more than a visitor to their family.

Each year during his visits, Eliudi would sit down with the family and discuss what had happened during the previous year. One year the problem that was deliberated was that the children were bringing home popular recorded music that had questionable lyrics. Roger describes the music as being on the "strong end of terrible." As a result Eliudi sat all five kids down and had each child tell him about their music.

Then Eliudi went to each child's room and asked, "What music do you own that Jesus would not want you to listen to? What music do you have that you could not play if Jesus was listening to the music with you?" Each of the kids was then asked to go through their music library and give up any questionable music cassettes to Eliudi. (This was a time before CDs were available.) Eliudi collected a big bag of cassettes and informed the youngsters that he was going to get rid of the music. Jan suggested that they throw the cassettes into the trash. Eliudi indicated that he believed that remedy was not good enough. He felt that someone else might retrieve the music and listen to it. To prevent that from happening, the cassettes were smashed beyond salvaging and thrown into a dumpster.

When Godwin first arrived in Oregon, Jan introduced him to people as, "This is Godwin from Africa. He is staying with us while he is attending high school." To make introductions easier, Jan started to remove selected words from the introductions. The introduction became, "This is our son from Africa." Finally Jan said, "This is our son, Godwin." As the George family started falling in love with Godwin and calling him their own, the qualifying causes just fell away. The differences in skin tone just disappeared with love and respect bonding the relationships between siblings and parents.

Before Godwin graduated from high school in 1989, Eliudi asked the

Georges to consider keeping Godwin and assisting him through college. Roger and Jan agreed with that proposal, but felt the need to take Godwin back to Tanzania and to reacquaint him with his roots. The Georges felt that Godwin was becoming a little too "American." They notified Eliudi that they were bringing Godwin home for a two month stay. Roger and Jan paid for their own airplane tickets to Africa while a friend paid for Godwin's ticket.

Since Jan was a nurse, she planned to help the people at Eliudi's school in Sakila with any of their medical needs. It seemed that Jan's longtime dream of a foreign mission trip was finally going to come true.

CHAPTER 10:
HEAL PEOPLE EVERYWHERE
(Luke 9:6)

The trio flew to Africa in 1990. If moving to America was traumatic for Godwin, going to Tanzania was also a huge adjustment for the Georges. Even though there were some primitive living conditions, Roger and Jan fell in love with the people. They found that the people of Sakila were very gracious and would give you anything that you required if it was theirs to give. The people did not have a lot, but they were willing to share.

The visit helped Roger and Jan to better understand Godwin's background and Eliudi's place in the village. When Eliudi was in America he was fun-loving and outgoing. When he was in Africa he was mostly business. This is a result of Eliudi's tremendous responsibility and respect in Tanzania. These factors underlined his huge influence in that country.

Godwin slept in his old room in his parent's house, while the Georges slept in a room provided by Eliudi. The house had no electricity, running water or inside kitchen. There was an outside pit toilet. A room next to the toilet had a bucket of water in it for bathing. Even if the conditions were rustic, every evening the family gathered for worship songs, to give thanks and for prayer.

Since Jan was going to be in Africa for two months, she wanted to put her nursing skills to good use at the School of Evangelism. Roger and Jan each brought two suitcases to Sakila. Two were packed with clothes and personal things, while the other suitcases were full of medical supplies. After conferring with Eliudi about a place to set up the medical practice, he provided a room for them to use and had it cleaned out. When the school staff brought in some tables and chairs, Jan got to work organizing supplies.

At first, Jan was going to doctor only the IEC staff, teachers and students who were attending the school in Sakila. Then one Sunday morning during church, Eliudi announced that the health clinic would be open to all who needed medical care, and that treatment would be free. On the following Monday, Jan was flooded with people who desired help. There were more than one hundred people in line at her door each day after that. Some days, Roger was able to help his wife. However, most of the time just Jan and a local helper manned the clinic.

In 1990 sub-standard medical practices were common in Tanzania. Since the country currently ranks 139th in the world in health care expenditures for its citizens, the life expectancy of a Tanzanian is only 53 years of age. For every one million people in Tanzania, there are just eight physicians.

From her experience Jan knew that medical personnel in the United States were regulated with standard rules and protocol. In Tanzania, no one cared about your medical diploma or license. If you were willing to help the people medically, they were willing to let you try. Jan discovered that she had to be adventuresome and very inventive when it came to treating patients. All manner of medical ailments showed up each day at the clinic. Two of the most common complaints were intestinal parasites and reoccurring malaria cases.

The dimensions of the building that Roger and Jan used for a clinic was about 30 x 40 feet. During the day, it was filled with people wanting to get medical help. Even a Muslim man came looking for help at the Christian-run clinic. After he received it, he told Eliudi that what was happening at the clinic was truly from God.

Eliudi visited the clinic soon after it opened. Even though he was not medically inclined, he saw that his people were hurting and required help. He said that he did not realize that his people had such a great need. At that point, the medical work in Sakila truly began.

As Jan began to consult people about their medical issues, she discovered that she needed additional medications for malaria, intestinal worms, infection and the like. Not knowing where to turn, Eliudi took Jan to a "so-called-doctor" in Arusha for advice. He seemed to have only a minimal education and questionable ethics. However, Jan was able to purchase some malaria medicine from him. Only on the way back to Sakila did Jan realize that medicine was outdated. That was the last time she would consult with that doctor!

Later, one incident occurred that really impacted Roger, Jan and Eliudi.

Jan had run out of medicine to treat intestinal worms. Because the patients desperately sought the medication, the Sakila staff had to bar the clinic doors. People were crying and begging, sticking their hands in the clinic's windows and trying to get in the building. Jan asked Eliudi to share with the disappointed crowd that she would find more deworming medication, and Jan assured those outside the clinic, through Eliudi, that no one would be left out! At this point Eliudi stated, "I did not know my people were hurting so much." During that first trip, Jan was finally able to find a reputable pharmacist who could provide good advice and an adequate supply of medications.

Before the Georges left for America, Eliudi and Jan went to the national government of Tanzania and filled out the paperwork necessary to officially establish a health clinic in Sakila. However, when the Georges left to return to Oregon, there was no one available to take their place at the clinic.

The following winter when Eliudi was making his American tour, he talked to Jan about what they could do to get the clinic back open and operating. Jan said that she could work from her end to get the word out that medical workers were desperately needed and direct them where they could go to help out. Even though this information was communicated to anyone who would listen, the medical work was slow to gain momentum.

Initially Jan became a medical coordinator to ease the way for anyone who could go to Sakila. She printed handouts that indicated the procedures required to obtain legal documents, lists of medications to take and information about what they might encounter in Tanzania. Once a medical team made the trip to Sakila, Jan expected them to find their way back on their own.

Roger and Jan did not return to Tanzania until 1997. By then Eliudi had built a small building that was to be used only as a clinic. It had three-rooms and by American standards was very primitive. The building had no lights, electricity or running water. It was cleanable as it had a cement floor and a tin roof. However, the eve between the roof and the walls was open enough that birds and rodents could enter the building. Large portions of the medical supplies had to be thrown away as rats would chew or defecate on those supplies. Even with these sub-standard conditions, the medical work progressed because of the Christian love the medical teams had for the people.

While Jan was in Tanzania she discovered that there was an American doctor who lived in Arusha by the name of Megan Joyce whose job it was to evacuate any non-national out of Tanzania if they became ill or injured. Dr. Joyce's husband, Allan, was a general practitioner and a surgeon. Together the Joyce's operated a health clinic in Arusha. From Dr. Megan Joyce, Jan was able to learn where she could get a good quantity and quality of medications and other supplies in Tanzania.

The incident that finally brought the medical mission in Sakila to the forefront occurred in 2002 shortly after Roger and Jan arrived home from another trip to Sakila. Like most countries outside of the United States, soccer is an extremely popular sport in Tanzania. Some of the teenagers and young adults in Sakila played on a soccer team, with Eliudi and Helen's youngest son, Steven, being a member of that team. One day the 40 member team was leaving Sakila on a large flatbed trailer that was being pulled by a farm tractor. As the tractor was traveling down the steep grade from Sakila, the trailer carrying the team somehow flipped over on a hairpin curve and eight of the teenage boys were killed outright, with three more of the boys dying on the way to the hospital. Steven lay badly injured and unconscious from a concussion.

Bishop Eliudi and his brother Joe were driving back to Sakila from Arusha on that Sunday afternoon after conducting church services there and were one of the first to arrive at the accident scene. In fact they arrived just minutes after the accident happened at a little past 3 o'clock. The scene that met them was a grizzly one. Eliudi immediately sent word to Sakila that there had been a horrible accident involving the soccer team. The villagers rushed down to the scene of the accident and were heartbroken at what they saw. Grieving parents picked up the bodies of the dead to carry them home. It took three hours to get all the injured boys to the hospital.

Eliudi said that he knew that Steven had been hurt but he could not make himself go over to see how serious his condition was. He certainly did not want to know that Steven had been killed. Even when Eliudi was told that Steven was still alive, he could not bring himself to look at his son. Eliudi's heart was broken over the tragedy. Instead of going to the hospital with Steven, Eliudi went home mentally shaken and physically sick to his stomach. He says that when he lay down on his bed at around 5 o'clock, the Lord put him into a deep sleep that lasted all night long, healing him.

Thirty kilometers away at the public hospital in Arusha, Steven was laid on a bed and an IV was started. That hospital in Arusha had a reputation as a place to go if you wanted to die. The hospital periodically closed for days because they did not have enough medical supplies or a sufficient quantity of staff to operate the facility.

Early the following morning after the accident, Eliudi was at the bed side of his injured son. For two days, no doctor came to examine the boy. Steven lay there all that time with no more medical treatment than the IV. Eliudi stayed with Steven and even had to change Steven's clothes and bedding when he soiled them.

Eliudi turned to the only person that he knew who had any real medical training - Jan George. He called and explained to Jan that Steven had been in a terrible accident, was in the hospital and the staff at the hospital seemed unwilling or unable to help the boy. What should he do?

Jan immediately told Eliudi to find Dr. Joyce and have her and her husband examine the boy. Eliudi hung up the phone and went to find Allan and Megan Joyce. Providentially, they were available and rode with Eliudi to the hospital. Since the hospital would not like non-staff doctors examining their patients, the Joyces went in as family friends. They took one look at Steven and told Eliudi that he had to get Steven out of that hospital at once as he may not live another day.

Megan Joyce contacted an airplane pilot who would fly Steven to a hospital in Kenya and instructed the pilot at what time to meet them at the Arusha Airport. Eliudi and the Joyces basically kidnapped Steven from the hospital and took him to the airport. Even though the hospital was furious over the proceedings, they sent a nurse to watch over Steven on the ride to the airport.

When Steven was placed in the plane and Eliudi had buckled himself into the passenger seat, the pilot took off. On the flight to the Kenyan hospital,

Eliudi and the pilot talked to each other to pass the time. Eliudi naturally shared with the pilot about his mission campus in Sakila.

When Steven was delivered to the hospital in Nairobi, the nurse at the check-in desk told Eliudi that he had to pre-pay $5,000 for Steven's care. She also stated that if pre-payment was not posted, Steven could not be admitted. Of course, Eliudi never had that much money on him. As a result, he became quite concerned about what to do next to save the life of his youngest son.

The pilot who had flown Steven and Eliudi to Kenya interrupted the admission stalemate and gave the nurse his credit card. He said whatever Eliudi's son needed, put it on his credit card. The pilot, who had only known Eliudi for the length of the flight, had enough confidence in his trustworthiness that he was willing to help Steven. The pilot knew that somehow Eliudi would pay him back.

Steven was in the Kenyan hospital for more than two months, and he did recover. He had to relearn how to walk, talk and write. After much prayer and therapy, Steven was back to living his normal life. The Kenyan hospital bill was paid for by concerned supporters in America.

From this incident, Eliudi focused harder on the medical portion of his mission. Once something had happened to a member of his family, it became deeply personal. He saw what good medicine could do for those in need of it.

Eliudi bought some land and planned to build a hospital east of Kikatiti. A portion of the basic building structure was constructed, but the funds seemed to run out for completing the hospital. The medical work was then scaled back to establishing a new, but bigger, workable clinic in Sakila.

During that time, the old clinic in the village was reopened and a full time Tanzanian woman by the name of Paulina Moses was employed at the facility in 2007. She had no formal medical training other than about a year of hands-on practice at a Catholic mission. However, Paulina does a good job of dispensing medications and dressing wounds. In 2014 Paulina was still at work six days a week administering first aid whenever the need arose. She has recently received schooling to train her as a clinical assistant. Even though the clinic was basically a full-time, first aid station, it makes a big difference in Sakila. The health of the people in the surrounding village has improved over the years due mainly to the presence of the little clinic and visiting medical teams.

Currently there are four medical teams that go almost yearly to Tanzania, departing from various locations in the United States. Initially Jan coordinated their dispatching to make sure that there is only one team in Sakila at a time. She informed the teams to take as much over-the-counter medicines as they possibly could to Tanzania. Those types of medicines are very expensive in Africa. At this point, the prescription medicines can be bought in-country for reasonable prices. (Tanzania has socialized medicine.)

For three weeks in 2011, Jan took a doctor with her to Sakila. He performed numerous operations such as tumor removals and minor hernia corrections with marvelous success rates. Not only did they practice in Sakila, but they also established schedules when they would visit surrounding villages.

To further the medical work in Sakila, Eliudi bought two acres of land across the road from the evangelism school where he has constructed a new clinic building. That structure really resembles a mini-hospital. The new clinic is situated outside of the IEC campus. This location is thought to be more convenient for the local community. The drop in foot traffic would reduce the chances of contagious diseases coming to the School of Evangelism campus where the first clinic building was located.

Even though the interior of the new clinic is not complete, there will be two surgery rooms, a laboratory, a portable x-ray machine, a pharmacy, and four examination rooms. A conference room will be used during the week for women's ministries, nutrition and well-baby classes. At this point the outside walls are constructed with windows and doors installed. The roof is on. A covered outside waiting area for patients is complete. The work to finish the interior of the clinic is progressing. Eventually equipment and supplies will be gathered to stock the clinic. In 2014 a small portion of the new clinic building was complete enough to move the clinic operations from the original building and start using the new building to receive patients.

As Jan looks ahead, she hopes someday to have an airstrip near the clinic so that medical teams can fly to distant villages where their skills are also needed

Research by the World Health Organization states that each year in Africa 30 million women become pregnant. Out of that number approximately

250,000 women die from pregnancy related causes. Also each year, approximately 590,000 babies die from stillbirth or complications from birth. There are 50 million orphans in Tanzania due to AIDS, war or the high rate of death of the mother during the birthing process. One year while Jan was ministering in Sakila, the ladies in the village wrote a song and sang it in church. In it they stated that during Jan's stay, not a single baby or mother died in childbirth.

Through the years, various volunteers have witnessed healings and miracles at the clinic in Sakila. Prayer is the key to these events. When God is consulted, He does mighty things! Some preemie and starving babies that were not supposed to live are today healthy and strong. Parents who could not conceive came back to the clinic the following year to show off their newborn baby. Terrible infections were cured. Burns were healed quickly with little or no scarring. Surgeries were done with no loss of life. One baby was sent to Kenya for critical surgery that if it had not been performed the baby would surely have died. The cost for that surgery was covered by a family in Oregon. Many, many more stories and praise reports can be told but, in all of them, God gets all the glory!

CHAPTER 11:
KEEP YOUR LAMPS BURNING
(Luke 12:35)

Bob and Adele Smith were pastoring a small church on the Yakima Indian Reservation near Yakima, WA. In October of 1981 they attended the three-day Spiritual Leadership Conference in Mt. Herman, CA. Although it was a long drive from their home in Washington State, a number of well-known evangelists were speaking on topics that the Smiths wanted to learn more about.

When they were seated at their table, they noticed an African man who looked a little bewildered and perhaps a bit lost in the large crowd. Even though there were four hundred people at the conference, this African stood out. Bob decided to walk over to the gentleman and asked him if he would like to join them at their table. After Bob and Adele introduced themselves, the man told the couple that he was Eliudi Issangya from Tanzania.

Despite the fact that his English was hard to understand, the Smiths took an immediate liking to this farmer-turned-preacher from Africa. After the conference speeches were concluded for the evening, Bob, Adele and Eliudi talked late into the night. Before they left the conference hall, the Smiths invited Eliudi to come to Yakima to speak to the congregation at their church.

A short time later Eliudi was in Yakima addressing Bob Smith's church. His vision for God's work in Africa was well received by Pastor Bob and Adele's congregation. That Sunday after Eliudi's talk, the church youth group had an outing to a local roller skate facility. Although Eliudi was wearing a suit, he laced up a pair of roller skates on his feet and attempted to learn to skate with the kids. When he tumbled once to the floor of the rink, Eliudi decided that skating was not for him.

While staying with Bob and Adele, Eliudi would entertain the Smith's two young daughters. He called them his "little angels." Bishop Eliudi has a soft spot in his heart for children. Of course, the girls adored him in return.

Before Eliudi traveled to his next speaking engagement, Bob and Adele wrote down what information they could so that they could keep in touch with Eliudi and follow the progress of his ministry. Eliudi gave the Smiths all the mailing information that he could and the address of his sponsoring church in Mariposa.

Soon after Eliudi's visit, Bob Smith took a pastoral position at the Bainbridge Christian Assembly on Bainbridge Island. That island is across the Puget Sound, west of Seattle, WA.

With the memories of Eliudi still fresh in their minds, they felt that they wanted to send some supplies to Sakila for the school. From their closet, they found an empty shoe box and filled it with new wooden pencils and ball point pens. The box was shipped to Africa at a cost that far exceeded the value of the contents. The Smiths were very gratified when they received word that the box had finally arrived safely at the school.

When Eliudi came back to America the following year, the invitation for him to speak at Bob's new church was offered and accepted. On his swing though the Pacific Northwest, Eliudi visited Bainbridge Island. During that stay, the shipping of supplies to Tanzania was one of the topics that Bob discussed with Eliudi. It was decided that Bob should contact the churches in California which were using metal shipping containers to send supplies to Sakila. Maybe those containers had enough extra room for the donations from Bob's church.

After determining that space was available, the Smiths drove a pickup load of supplies their first year to the loading site from their home in Washington State. The following year, they took another pickup load to San Francisco, California. Only that time, they had a trailer hitched to their pickup which was also full of essential mission materials. Even with the cheaper means of bulk shipping to Sakila, a way to substantially reduce the shipping cost even more was desired.

Through contacts, Bob Smith found that containers leaving the Seattle area were considerably cheaper than those leaving from the San Francisco Bay ports. After a group conference that included Bishop Eliudi, the 1985 container loading was moved to Bainbridge Island and eventually to Poulsbo, WA. That location required the churches from California and four other states to transport their donations all the way to Washington State.

Shipping from Washington State allowed the Smith's church members to ship more mission materials to Sakila. They would spend the entire year collecting and storing items in boxes and plastic bags for the springtime loading. And every year Eliudi would come to Bob and Adele's church during container loading to give an update on the progress being made for God in Sakila.

In 1990 Bob went with a group of workers to build a teacher residence in Sakila. Bob not only had a great time on the trip, but he also came back with a fire in his heart for the work being done there. This was the first time that Bob had ever been in a third world culture. He found the experience amazing and very rewarding. Bob was astounded at the people's Christian joy. Even though they had a difficult life, they loved Jesus Christ and wanted to spread the gospel.

As he went to sleep in Sakila at night, he would listen to bats flying though the rafters of the building. He would think about the conditions that the evangelism students were then encountering on a daily basis. The students had wooden, twin-sized bunk beds to sleep on. However, at the time there were not enough bunks for each student to have his own bed. One student would sleep on the top of the wooden bunk and two students would sleep on the bottom bed. (There were no mattresses at that time for the students to lie on.) Each week the student on the top bed would change places with a person on the bottom bed. Then the next week the person who had slept doubled up on the bottom bed for two weeks would be moved to the top bunk. If a pupil preferred not to sleep in a bunk with another fellow student, he slept on the cement floor on a flattened cardboard box as a cushion. Of course sleeping on the floor subjected the student to all kinds of crawling insects, hopping frogs and creeping geckos. Eliudi explained, "This is an example of how much the students want to learn about the gospel of Jesus Christ."

At the yearly school reunion conferences in Sakila, the spirit refocuses and energizes the attendees. As an example, when the offering is taken, the students come forward to leave their shoes and watches on the alter. "They give all that they have back to God. Nothing is held in reserve," Bob says. "To see this is viewing the power of God at work."

In 1992 Jan George encouraged Godwin to go with Bishop Eliudi on his American tour to visit his supporting churches. When Eliudi left Oregon, Godwin was with his father and traveled to Bainbridge Island. They stopped at Bob Smith's church to give a progress report. Godwin, on the other hand, met one of Bob and Adele's grown-up daughters by the name of Kim. She was one of Eliudi's "little angels" that he had entertained when they were younger. When Godwin returned to Oregon, he told his American brothers that he had met the girl that he wanted to marry. This started a multi-year, long-distance relationship between Kim and Godwin.

When the Christian Fellowship in Mariposa ceased to operate in 1993, Eliudi was left without a sponsoring church. He contacted Bob and Adele to ask them to be his American sponsor. Bob agreed and has been sponsoring Eliudi's visits to the United States ever since. After the invitation letter was written in the 1990s and Bishop Eliudi had arrived in America, US Customs would telephone Bob Smith to make sure that Eliudi was who he said he was. Current custom agents look into their computer to see that Eliudi has visited this country many times and has always returned to Tanzania when he said that he would. Verification telephone calls from US Customs are no longer required.

In that same year of 1993, Bishop Eliudi's sponsoring churches in the United States decided that instead of having Eliudi's mission under one church's umbrella; it should be a stand-alone operation. U.S. government forms were filled out to designate the Sakila mission as a non-profit organization. After approval, the International Evangelism Outreach (IEO) organization was formed to complement and support the work done in Africa. Being long-time supporters from Mariposa, Judy and Garven Kinley were chosen as the IEO information coordinators with Judy becoming the treasurer.

The year 1994 brought about a change in Bob and Adele's life. Eliudi's son

Godwin traveled to Bainbridge Island and asked Bob if he could marry his daughter. Bob and Adele were excited about the leading of the Lord in the relationship between Godwin and Kim. With Bob's blessing, Godwin proposed marriage to Kim one night at a restaurant where Kim excitedly accepted the proposal.

The wedding was performed on February 17, 1996 at what is now Gateway Fellowship in Poulsbo, WA. This wedding was a ceremony to remember with hundreds of guests in attendance. The three fathers officiated the wedding. Roger George presided over the first third of the wedding ceremony. Bob Smith conducted the middle portion and Bishop Eliudi concluded the wedding speaking in English, Swahili and the tribal language of Meru.

After that ceremony, the couple flew to Sakila and had a second wedding for their friends and relatives living in Tanzania. Since a wedding ceremony in Africa is a time of great celebration, Godwin and Kim wanted everyone there to share in the wedding festivities. On May 25, 1996 another wedding ceremony was conducted at the school's church in Sakila. After the second wedding, Godwin and Kim moved into a house in Sakila. When they were expecting their first baby in 1997 they came back to Poulsbo, WA to take advantage of American health care facilities. They returned to Sakila in January of 1998 to live once again in Sakila. When the second child was expected in 1999, the couple relocated to Poulsbo. Godwin and Kim then decided to stay in the Poulsbo area after the birth of their second daughter. Kim and Godwin now have three daughters. Since Bishop Eliudi needed a trusted contact in the United States, Godwin became that person.

Bob has been back to Sakila numerous times. Being a pastor, his passion is for the School of Evangelism. He feels that there are a lot of improvements that need to be accomplished in Sakila. At this time the dormitory rooms that house the students have only a few light bulbs dangling from electrical wires. Those bulbs are the only lighting that the students have to study by. In addition, there is no ceiling in the building. The students hang their clothes from the electrical wires that extend across the rafters to the light bulbs. As a retired electrician, Bob finds these conditions unacceptable.

He would also like to see rock or cement pathways laid between the campus buildings. During the rainy season, the sticky mud around the school clings to everyone's shoes. Even though there are steel shoe scrapers outside each doorway, mud still tracks into the buildings.

In 1998 Bob Smith left the church on Bainbridge Island to pastor the New Covenant Fellowship Church at Port Gamble, WA. (That town is near Poulsbo, WA.) Before he took over the new church, Adele and Bob went to Sakila for nine weeks of missionary work.

After Adele and Bob had been in Sakila for a week, they prepared to do some of their laundry. Eliudi told them, "You should not be the ones to wash your clothes. Place the dirty laundry outside your door and someone from the village would do it for you." Bob and Adele indicated that they were perfectly capable of cleaning their own clothes. They felt that they really did not want to be a burden to anybody. Eliudi looked them lovingly in the eyes, "You came all the way here from America to minister to these people. There is very little that they can give to you in return. Please, do not rob them of this simple act of service to you." To that, Bob and Adele agreed that someone in the village could wash their clothes.

The people of Tanzania know that they wrestle with spirits not made of flesh and blood. Witchdoctors and demons are a reality that the people deal with on a continual basis.

Every Wednesday at the Bible School, the students, teachers and some of the visiting guests would spend the middle part of the day in fasting and prayer. The Holy Spirit's presence is felt in a mighty way during those times and lays gloriously on everyone in attendance. On one Wednesday, Bob was on the way back to the conference hall after a short break at Eliudi's house. As he walked on the path, a demon-possessed teenaged girl was walking on the same path but going in the opposite direction. During previous occasions she had demonically raged with unholy speech and did unspeakable things to herself and others. The school staff had been working unsuccessfully with her to dispel her demons. Bob did not know the girl or anything about her condition. As they passed each other on the path, they lightly brushed against each other. The teenage girl immediately fell like a rock, unconscious.

A few of the near-by school staff hurriedly picked her up and rushed her to a location where they could safely lay her down. Then they prayed fervently over her. When she recovered, the evil possession that had inhabited her for years was totally gone. She had been set free of those malevolent spirits. Bob confides that it was not anything that he had done to heal the girl. He believed that the Holy Spirit was saturating him so completely after praying and fasting that day with the school students that as soon as she touched him, the Spirit jumped to her body from his and healed her. Bob had never experienced anything like that in his life. He wept in joy at the miracle that had happened through him for this teenage girl.

The students of the Bible School fast and pray for their sponsors in America. They would not have the current facilities or teachers if it were not for those who support and donate to the school. In truth, they pray for Americans more than Americans pray for them. The students want to serve the body of Christ and they do not want to stop serving. They know that their sponsors are a vital part of their spreading the gospel in Africa.

It is Bob's vision and prayer that Christians here in the United States will come to see an outpouring of God's Spirit to the level that is being experienced in other parts of the world. He believes that God is doing great things and Bob wants this country to be in the very center of that outpouring. Bob also prays that he will be alive and rejoicing when we see that day approaching. He says that the ministry in Tanzania is all about Christ's command to his disciples found in Matthew 28:19 and 20; "*Therefore go and make disciples of all nations, baptizing them in the name of the Father and of the Son and of the Holy Spirit; and teaching them to obey everything I have commanded you. And surely I am with you always, to the very end of the age.*" Bob concludes, "God is so good."

CHAPTER 12:

LET THOSE WHO THIRST, COME
(Isaiah 55:1)

In January of 1995 Bishop Eliudi was in the United States once again and on a tour of churches who were supporting various causes connected with his ministry. For a man who lives almost on the Equator in Africa, visiting Montana in January was not the most comfortable place to be. While in the frigid northlands, Eliudi was cold all the time. No matter where he went, he was cold. Not even the love and respect that he was shown by his long-time supporters could warm his body. One frigid day he found himself riding over bleak, snow covered roads in Southern Montana. Eliudi was riding with Jack Reinmuth and they were on their way to Broadus, MT. That town was not very big and it was dwarfed by the surrounding big sky country.

Jack Reinmuth had been persistently calling his friend Elder Justin Mader of the Family Life Church in Gillette, WY. He had explained to Justin that he had met a man from Tanzania who was doing some fantastic work over there. He believed that Justin's church might be able to assist in that work in some way. In the early 1990s Justin had talked to his pastor, Marty Crump, about having Eliudi Issangya visit their church. Things moved rather slowly at first. Then in 1994, the visitation was finally scheduled for January of the next year. So it was that Pastor Marty drove the 110 miles from Gillette to Broadus to meet Eliudi and transport him to Gillette.

As Pastor Marty drove north to Broadus, he was wondering what Eliudi looked like and what sort of man he was. The only thing Pastor Marty knew was that he was to meet Jack and Eliudi at a restaurant in Broadus. When Pastor Marty arrived in town, he easily found the meeting location and sat down in the warm café to wait for their impending arrival. Shortly, a white man and a black man entered the restaurant. Right away Pastor Marty knew these were the people he was there to meet.

During introductions, Pastor Marty bought everyone a cup of hot coffee to warm them after the winter drive and to get acquainted. After the initial contact was concluded, Jack said goodbye and left Eliudi in Pastor Marty's care. Marty and Eliudi bundled up to ward off the cold and left the café. They climbed into Marty's pickup and started the drive south to Wyoming. Eliudi certainly did not know Pastor Marty and he only vaguely knew where he was. He was once again taking a giant leap of faith and just going where God led him.

On the way to Gillette, Marty asked Eliudi about his life and work in Africa, comparing Eliudi's responses to his own experiences in America. Like everyone, Pastor Marty took an instant liking to Eliudi. The African was undoubtedly tired and cold from his long winter trip. He would take cat naps every so often to catch up on his sleep. When Pastor Marty arrived at his home in Gillette, he showed his guest a cozy, warm room where Eliudi would be sleeping during his visit.

On Sunday, Bishop Eliudi spoke during the service at Family Life Church and shared the overall view of his ministry in Sakila. After the service a collection was taken to support Eliudi and his work. Jack Reinmuth picked Eliudi up on Monday and drove him to Scotts Bluff, NE where he had another speaking engagement. Every year after that first contact, Eliudi came back for a visit at Family Life Church and gave progress reports of the work being planned or accomplished in Africa.

In 1998 Family Life Church sent Justin Mader, Jack Reinmuth and three others to Tanzania to look over the school in Sakila and other projects that Eliudi was promoting. They came back with very favorable reports and recommended that the church continue to donate to the mission.

In January of 1999 Eliudi was again visiting cold, wind-swept Gillette, WY and speaking at the Family Life Church. That year Michele and Brian Kennedy volunteered to drive him to Billings, MT to catch an airplane to his next destination. On the way, Michele asked Eliudi what was his most pressing need in Tanzania. He said the thing they desired most was some deep, reliable wells that produced clean, drinkable water. Michele looked at Eliudi with disbelief, "Bishop Eliudi, I know someone who drills wells for a living. He happens to be my father. However, at this point he is not a Christian." In true Eliudi fashion, he replied, "At this time, your father's lack of faith is not a vital factor. We will simply pray to God and He will change your father's heart."

When Eliudi came back to Gillette in 2000, Michele and Brian had a dinner party at their house for Eliudi and invited Michele's parents, Trusty and Marilyn Matheson. No one knew how the meeting between her well-drilling father and Eliudi would go as Trusty had a reputation for being rather cantankerous. After dinner, Eliudi sat down with Trusty, detailed his mission in Sakila and asked him if he would be willing to come to Africa in order to drill for water. To Trusty's and everyone's surprise, he said that he would really like to do that.

Then the well driller learned that he would have to ship one of his own drilling rigs to Tanzania as there were none available in Sakila. As everyone who knew Trusty Matheson was aware, he was a practical businessman. He asked, "If I ship my rig over there, are you going to ship it back? Better yet, can someone over there buy it so that it can just stay there?" Trusty was willing to help others, but he was justifiably concerned about the finances involved with the project. Matheson Drilling had only two drilling rig trucks. This project to drill the wells in Africa would take 50% of his projected income away. Eliudi's answer should sound familiar, "Let us just pray about it. God will work it out."

When Eliudi came back the following year, the Holy Spirit had worked in Trusty's life and he had given his heart to God and he was anxiously waiting to meet Eliudi that January. There was no more talk about who would pay for the drilling rig. Trusty and his new church, Family Life, would do what it could to ship the rig to Sakila and drill those wells that were so desperately needed.

Before the rig and the supplies were shipped to Tanzania, Pastor Marty, church member David Kidd and Trusty went to Sakila to survey the land where the wells were to be drilled. Examining the wells that Bruce Crower had drilled years before, Trusty discovered that the wells were played out and that clean water was again difficult to obtain in Sakila.

While they were there, Bishop Eliudi and the Family Life delegation met with officials of the Tanzanian government. The Family Life members explained to the politicians that their church would drill the water wells for free. However, they wanted the national government to admit the drilling rig truck and supplies into the country duty free. This was to be a humanitarian effort and they wanted to accomplish it as frugally as possible.

Also, the group from the church wanted the Tanzanian government to have power lines run to the area so that electric pumps could be utilized to supply the water. The politicians that were at the meeting were excited at the prospect of clean water for the people and readily agreed to both demands.

Pastor Marty also asked Eliudi if his people would build a garage to house the drilling rig; they were more than happy to do so. Pastor Marty gave Eliudi the funds from his church for the garage materials and relied on Eliudi's workers to accomplish the construction.

During a meeting at the Sakila church, Pastor Marty pledged to the village people that his crew was there to get them water by drilling wells for them. Trusty was not so optimistic about that promise and asked Pastor Marty when they were alone, "How do you even know if there is water there to tap into?" Pastor Marty said that they would just have to trust in God to bring in the water.

Church member David Kidd also quietly lamented to Pastor Marty, "You promised these people water. We are a long ways from being able to deliver on that promise." Marty responded, "Some of the people in surrounding villages are packing water for eight miles one way for their daily needs. They have to carry the containers on their heads or on the backs of donkeys to get the water to their homes. Some of the water that they retrieve is from a mud hole in which animals have waded. We have no choice but to deliver on this promise." With that, the water well project was given the approval to proceed.

Back in Wyoming, Trusty picked out one of his two rigs to send to Tanzania. The truck certainly was not a new one. In fact in 1986, Trusty had drilled 665,000 feet of wells with the rig. However he had the truck reworked, new tires installed and a coat of fresh paint was applied. He even put a new seat in the cab. Everything that could be greased was thoroughly greased. Since he had owned the truck, it had never been in such good shape.

Per an agreement, Trusty would donate the drilling rig, but the church would have to provide the money to ship it to Tanzania along with the supplies and materials required to drill the wells. To this end, the little church raised $60,000 in nine months. One person, who had talked to Eliudi about the water situation in 1983, was Clarice Wallin of Bozeman, MT. When she heard of the water project being conducted by the Gillette church, she generously contributed to the shipping of the drilling rig.

The cost of shipping the drilling rig to Tanzania was $18,000. Since the drilling truck was too big to fit into a shipping container, the church had to pay an extra amount for its shipping. Besides the truck, a 40 foot metal container would also be shipped to Sakila. It would contain all the pipe, drill heads, pumps, electrical wire and tools needed to complete the wells.

In 2002, the rig had to be driven from Wyoming to Galveston, TX to be loaded on a cargo ship. Trusty and three other men from the church started on their journey and delivered the drilling truck. After they arrived in Galveston, the men purchased a shipping container and loaded it with the required drilling equipment, well supplies and boring tools. Hand tools were put into metal boxes on the drilling rig with the lids of the boxes welded shut. An agreement with the shipping company was made that the drilling truck would be stored below deck for the voyage to Africa. If the truck was set on the weather deck, Trusty was worried about what salt water spray would do to the truck and its drilling rig.

Since Trusty and his crew wanted to be in Dar es Salam, Tanzania when the ship carrying the truck and metal container arrived, they hurried home from Galveston and watched the ship's progress. The ship first sailed to Belgium where the drilling rig and the container with the supplies were off-loaded. Those items were reloaded onto another ship bound for Africa. Only this time, the drilling rig was positioned on the weather deck. The ship was supposed to travel through the Suez Canal but for some reason went on a longer trip around the Cape of Good Hope.

When the ship's arrival date drew near, Trusty and his wife, Marilyn, along with son-in-law, Brian Kennedy, and fellow church member, David Kidd, flew to the Kilimanjaro Airport and were met by Eliudi in his Land Rover. When the group arrived in Sakila, the people of the village were overjoyed to see them. Trusty was happy to see that a garage had been constructed large enough to house the drilling rig. The next day, Eliudi drove Trusty and his crew the 600 kilometers to Dar es Salam to claim the rig.

The ship carrying the drilling rig and container docked in Dar es Salam a week before Trusty arrived in Africa. However at the pier, Trusty found out that the port authority in Dar es Salam wanted some tariff money to release the rig from their holding compound. Since Trusty and his group had been promised that no import tariff would be levied and since they did not have the money that was being asked to release the drilling truck, they were quietly furious over the request.

After much fruitless discussion with the port officials, Trusty requested that if he could not take possession of the rig at that time, he wanted to at least be allowed to inspect it. He was told that his request was out of the question. The tariff officers would not let Trusty near the truck. Negotiations quickly came to an impasse with nothing more being able to be accomplished that day. Since it was too far to drive back to Sakila, an overnight stay in Dar es Salam was necessary.

The travelers found a hotel on the waterfront that had affordable rooms available for everyone. Trusty and Marilyn soon found out that most American and African hotels have entirely different standards. On inspecting the rooms at the waterfront hotel, Marilyn was shocked at the conditions she found. Dark mold was everywhere on the walls of the bedrooms. The beds did have two sheets, of which neither was any too clean. There were no blankets or towels available. The mosquito net that once was had been white was dark brown from dirty hands opening and closing it. There was one bathroom for everyone on that floor to use. It was even moldier than the bedrooms. The plumbing in the bathrooms was constantly dripping water, with the stalls much too dirty to take a shower in anyway. (Dar es Salaam is one of the most humid cities on earth. That humidity contributes greatly to the growth of mold.)

Even with the deplorable conditions, Trusty and his group stayed that night at the waterfront hotel. Marilyn hardly slept at all during the night from worrying about what diseases they were coming in contact with. She got out of bed in the morning feeling horrible. The stress of the situation was weighing heavily on her and her companions.

On the second day in Dar es Salam, a different tack was taken with the port authorities. Eliudi knew a friend who worked for the government of Tanzania. That friend was quickly contacted concerning the situation and was told to remind the politicians that they had agreed to let the well drilling equipment into the country without tariffs. His message to the government was, "Please, quickly release the drilling equipment." Even though this seemed to be the only avenue that would get the rig freed, it did not look like the rig would be released on the second day.

With another night's stay looking like a real possibility, David Kidd declared that he was not going to stay another night in the "roach motel". He went to the New African Hotel, discovered that it was more agreeable to his Western standards and booked himself in. However, it cost a lot of money to stay there and Trusty and Marilyn had not brought an excess of cash along with them. Since Trusty was aware of his wife's stressed condition, he elected to splurge and also stay at the New African. Even with the cleaner hotel, the entire group was depressed and frustrated over their situation. Marilyn was beginning to wonder if God really was guiding their well drilling project.

That evening the group went to another hotel for supper. In the waiting room of the dining area, five different car license plates from the United States were hung on the wall. There in the middle was one from Wyoming and it was from the very county in which Gillette was located. Marilyn saw that plate as a little piece of home and a sign from God that things were going to be alright.

The next day dawned with the group having had a much better night's sleep. When they arrived at the port mid-morning, the truck still had not been released. Brian felt he had to do something. He walked along the outside of the port's chain link fence stopping every so often to pray to God. With his hands lifted toward heaven, he prayed out loud to Jesus for the truck and shipping container to be released. Everyone wondered if the modern-day walls of Jericho would finally fall. That afternoon, without any explanation, the drill rig was suddenly freed from the port compound.

Trusty finally was able to inspect his drilling rig. The body of the truck had minor cable chafing marks on it from being hoisted on and off the ships. He also discovered that the truck's battery was dead. It was thought that a deck hand or two had listened to the radio in the cab during the sea voyage and had depleted the battery. The tool boxes had been forced open and all the hand tools had been stolen. But since Trusty had painted and greased the rig before it left Gillette, the salt water spray had not deteriorated the rig to any noticeable extent.

At 3 o'clock in the afternoon, the truck was started and, with Eliudi leading the way in his Land Rover and Trusty driving his truck, they started the journey to Sakila. As they travelled, Trusty stayed right on Eliudi's rear bumper so that he would not lose Eliudi in the strange city. As they weaved in and out of the traffic, Eliudi waved wildly at the traffic cops to make sure that they did not delay the drilling rig.

On the road from Dar es Salam to Moshi and Sakila, there was a port of entry station. Since Eliudi thought that the drilling rig had been pre-cleared, they drove right through the check point without stopping. The Tanzanian police were soon in hot pursuit after the Land Rover and the drilling rig. Trusty's heart sank at the prospect of more trouble. Once the two vehicles were stopped, Eliudi was able to persuade the custom officer that the import fees had already been taken care of. With that incident resolved, the road trip continued on into the night.

When the small caravan pulled off of the main highway to take the side road up to Sakila, Eliudi decided that Trusty's big rig would not be able to negotiate the hairpin curve on the shortest route to Sakila. He informed the group that they would have to take the back way. The alternate road was longer and it was steep and contained many sharp curves, but no hairpin turns. As they traveled, the drilling rig labored up the grade and bellowed out a loud exhaust.

It was the middle of the night as the Land Rover and the truck neared Sakila. When they arrived, everyone in the village awoke to welcome the drilling truck. Because they had waited for two years for the truck's arrival, it was time for celebration. At 2 o'clock in the morning, the people of the village were dancing, singing, clapping and giving thanks to God for the promise of clean water.

The shipping container filled with drilling supplies arrived the next day. Since Brian Kennedy could not wait to get a well started, Trusty set his rig up near the School of Evangelism and started to drill. Within a few days, a new well was completed and producing water. Next, the rig was moved to the Crower Trade School and another well was dug. A third well was also completed that week at the school's farm. All too soon, it was time for Trusty and his drilling crew to fly back to Gillette.

CHAPTER 13:
I WAS THIRSTY AND YOU GAVE ME DRINK
(Matthew 25:35)

When Family Life Church started the well drilling project, they thought that they would go to Africa, drill three or four wells, come home and be done with the project. After their first successes, they knew that they had to return to Africa to continue helping those wonderful people. Trusty has been back to Tanzania many times and has completed 55 or 60 more wells since the first three were drilled. Now he has a crew of Sakila men who help him dig the wells. They work fine together as a team and take pride in their accomplishments. Besides teaching the men how to drill wells, Trusty feeds the helpers well.

The containers with the well drilling supplies are shipped each March to Tanzania from Poulsbo, WA. That means that in the months preceding the shipment, everything required has to be gathered and paid for. Each year, Family Life Church raises funds for the project by asking for donations of money and materials. Volunteers haul the materials in pickups and trailers to Washington State for loading in a shipping container.

God knew what He was doing when He had Pastor Marty pick up Bishop Eliudi in Montana on that cold January day in 1995 and drive him to his church. There are very few places in the United States that are better suited for supplying Sakila's requirements for clean water than Gillette, WY. In the immediate area there is a lot of energy production in the form of coal, uranium and natural gas. When a gas well has finished producing, the workings of the well are removed and the well is capped off. This results in a lot of used electrical wire being left over. The gas companies call Trusty and ask him if he could use the wire for his wells in Tanzania. Trusty gladly brings it home, inspects it for his use in Africa, and ships the good wire over.

One year the Weatherford Pump Company called Trusty and said they had heard that Trusty was digging wells for needy people in Africa. The company had discontinued a model of water pump and wondered if Trusty could use the remaining unsold pumps. Trusty informed the company that the pumps offered were exactly the models that he was using. Then he asked the pump representative how many he had. The answer was that he had 300 pumps that they could donate to the African project for free. Those pumps were sent to Tanzania in the next shipping container. After experiencing all of this outpouring, his wife Marilyn says, "Do you suppose God wants us to drill wells in Tanzania? The answer to that is pretty obvious."

Not only had the government of Tanzania failed at first to allow the drilling rig to past through customs without payment, but no electrical lines had been installed in outlying regions to power the water pumps. Gasoline generators were temporarily placed near the wells to provide the needed electricity. However, since fuel is very expensive in Tanzania, the generators could be operated only on a very limited basis. Even where power is available, some of the communities cannot afford to pay the electrical bill.

A town called Valeska had a drilled well but it, like other towns in rural Tanzania, was without electrical power. In the vicinity of Valeska there live about 4,000 people who have no clean water supply. Also in the town there is a public primary school staffed with four teachers, each instructing about one hundred students. However, the teachers do not stay in Valeska. They left not because of the class load but because there was no fresh water supply in the town.

In 2011, Trusty shipped enough solar panels to Tanzania for one well. He installed those panels and a solar pump in the Valeska well. But, he had to leave the job uncompleted as a part on the new solar equipment was defective. A replacement part was ordered, but it did not arrive in Africa before he left for home. A member of his native drilling team received and installed the new part and reported that the well worked satisfactory. The people in Valeska now have clean water. An American nurse who has visited the town stated that in one year, water borne diseases have diminished by 75% in that area because of the clean water from the well.

In 2012, 51 solar panels were purchased to power some of the other wells. Shallow water wells take a minimum of four solar panels to operate the pump. A deep well may take up to 12 panels for the same pump.

The question was asked of Trusty, "What do the people in the villages do when you bring in a well?" He replied, "At first, the people in the village do not really understand what you are doing there. You start drilling and you are using water to flush out the hole. Mud flows around the drilling area and they stare at you and the mud skeptically. Then you put a pump into the ground and turn it on. They are still not impressed because the first water that comes out is full of silt and dirt. Then when that clean, pure water starts to flow, you hear happier screaming and hollering than you ever thought possible."

When Trusty was asked, "Has all the hard work been worth it after expending so much of your time and energy to dig wells for people that you would never have known if you had not gone to Africa?" His answer was, "If the well drilling project has saved one life, it has been worth it. And we do not know how many lives we have saved or just made better. And when it comes down to it, it is a God thing. We have had to put up with a lot of disappointment from the politicians in Tanzania. Well, we do not do this for them. We drill wells for the people; the people we have come to love."

In Africa, Trusty has acquired the Swahili name of Baba Maji. In English that means "Father Water." It can be said that not all missionaries have to preach sermons to reach a population for Jesus. Or as St. Francis of Assisi commanded, "Preach the Gospel at all times and when necessary use words."

As for Matheson Drilling in Gillette, in 2002 50% of its drilling rigs were sent to Africa. Since then Trusty has enough new business in Gillette that he now has four drilling rigs working. His company has experienced a 400% increase in business since beginning Trusty's work in Tanzania.

During his 2009 trip, Trusty tried to dig a well in Same, Tanzania. Unfortunately, Trusty and his crew had drilled down 600 feet without hitting water. They would have gone deeper, but they ran out of drill pipe. To finish the well, more pipe would have to be shipped to Tanzania in next year's container.

The following year, Trusty decided to try to finish the well in Same. That unfinished well was 165 miles away from Sakila and it would take a lot of driving time to get there. However, Trusty really wanted to provide that village a good supply of clean water. When the rig was loaded with drilling pipe and supplies, Mandela, his Tanzanian helper, and Trusty started the engine and drove out of Sakila early in the morning.

Even though Trusty did not know all the local traffic laws, he felt safe driving his own rig in the Tanzanian traffic. When he drove out onto the paved Moshi to Arusha Highway, the trip got a lot smoother for the driver and passenger. Soon they were rolling along so well that Trusty drove right by a highway inspection station where he should have stopped to have his rig inspected.

Within seconds the Tanzanian police were in pursuit of Trusty and his drilling rig. Pulling to the side of the road, a frowning Trusty parked the truck. The traffic officer informed him of his transgression of not stopping at the station to have his rig inspected. No matter how Trusty explained the mistake to the officer, the policeman would not allow the truck to continue. The traffic officer stated that Tanzanian rules were rules that had to be followed. Reluctantly, Trusty agreed to return grudgingly to the inspection station.

At the check-point, the police found that the drilling truck was in good working order. Thinking that everything was settled, he got back into the truck and prepared to drive off. But no one would give them permission to leave. After setting at the inspection station for what seemed like hours, Mandela crawled up into the cab and said that he was told that they could leave. Trusty had had enough of sitting around and wasting time, so he started the engine and drove off in a hurry.

Before the truck was a kilometer down the road, the inspection police were again in pursuit. Miserably Trusty pulled over the side of the road once more. The police were really irritated this time. They wanted to know who gave him permission to leave the inspection area. Trusty could only shrug his shoulders and look dejected. The officer then told him that his truck would have to go back to the check-point to be ticketed.

At the inspection area, Trusty was written a ticket for $2,000 for fleeing an inspection point. (That ticket would equal $3,850,000 Tanzanian shillings.) To make matters worse the police wanted the penalty paid before the truck could leave.

No matter how much he reasoned with the Tanzanian police, they would not retract the ticket. It seemed that no one would listen to what Trusty had to say about what he considered a trivial matter. Drilling wells for people who had no water had to be more important than a minor communication failure that caused his truck to leave the check point before they had permission. As hard as he tried, he never did find out who have given Mandela the OK to leave the check-point.

Disgustedly, Trusty called Eliudi on the cell phone and explained what had happened. Eliudi told him to stay calm and remain where he was. Eliudi knew a number of contacts in the government that could convince the police to withdraw the ticket. However, that solution would take many wasted and frustrating hours.

Eventually it was decided that Eliudi would drive to the inspection site to pick up Trusty and bring him back to Sakila. Mandela would have to stay with the drilling rig to guard it through the night. Besides being stuck at a noisy check point, Mandela was bitten repeatedly by hungry mosquitos all night long.

Even when he was comfortably reclining in the passenger seat and traveling back to Sakila, Trusty was still in a foul mood. He was fed up with the Tanzanian police and its bureaucracy. He turned to Eliudi and quietly lamented, "Now I know why the British up and left Tanzania!"

Eliudi thought about that statement for a few seconds. He said that he then laughed for days after that at Trusty's frustration with the Tanzanian way of doing things. Eliudi was still laughing at the statement years later.

CHAPTER 14:
WHATEVER YOU DID FOR ONE OF THESE, YOU DID FOR ME
(Matthew 25:40)

While Bishop Eliudi was visiting Helena, MT in 1998, the Life Covenant Church was conducting a fund-raiser for the International Evangelism Outreach organization. In attendance at the gathering was Sami Butler, who is a registered nurse. She was impressed with Eliudi and his message and was delighted to be working with her church to help sustain his mission in Tanzania.

When she got a chance, Sami asked Eliudi if he ever allowed medical teams to come to Sakila to doctor the local people. He smiled really big at that question and said that he did indeed have medical teams that visited his village. He referred Sami to his San Diego ministry school classmate, Helen Johnson, who also lived in Helena. When Sami was able to meet with Helen, she had Sami place a telephone call to Jan George in Oregon to discuss the current medical outreach being conducted in Sakila. After talking with Jan for two hours, Sami was excited about what she had learned and of the possibility of being able to assist with the needs there.

Soon after her conversation with Jan, Sami started to organize a group of people for a journey to Tanzania. After juggling everyone's schedule, a travel date was set for the spring of 2002. However, those plans were thwarted when in September of 2001, the attack on the United States happened. During that unsettled time, a disappointing but necessary decision was made to postpone their travel plans.

It was not until July of 2005 that Sami organized and finally led a medical team to Sakila. Their group included seventeen members. It consisted of two doctors, two dentists, a periodontist, five nurses, an electrician and five support staff. (The electrician was included to wire the clinic building for overhead lights.)

Before the medical team left Helena, their church gave them some ministry money. Those funds would be used in Tanzania to purchase electrical and medicinal supplies, buy paint for the clinic, send patients for surgery that could not be accomplished at the clinic, provide for eye exams and glasses, and make food available for needy children.

After a series of very long flights, the volunteers finally arrived in Sakila late in the evening. At daylight, the team was able to finally see the medical clinic where they would be working. The building was made of cement blocks coated with stucco and divided into three small and dusty rooms. There was another smaller building behind the clinic that at one time had been used as sleeping quarters. That building was separated from the clinic by a narrow, covered breezeway. The visiting team converted that previous sleeping area into the dental treatment area.

The team spent the first day sorting through supplies which had been left by previous teams. Some of those supplies had become outdated and were dealt with accordingly. They found cardboard boxes and their contents which had been destroyed by the ravenous African insects. A general clean-up was conducted and existing supplies were organized.

Since the old clinic's main entry door led into the building's middle room, that room was used to screen incoming patients. There the initial vital signs and histories were taken and post-exam medications were distributed. The west room of the clinic became the exam room. It was divided into two compartments by a blanket that was suspended by a wire hung through the middle of the room. One doctor saw his patients in the front half of the room while another doctor saw her patients in the back half. The east room of the clinic was used as a treatment and storage room. In that room were two old exam tables and a mountain of cardboard boxes. This area was used to wash wounds, treat feet, give injections and conduct other similar procedures.

The team would have contact with 1,214 patients over the nine days that they were there in 2005. During their stay, the doctors treated mostly respiratory problems, ear and eye infections, asthma, goiters and elephantiasis of the feet and legs. From all the heavy physical labor that the people in the area accomplish, back and joint pain were common complaints, along with burns and lacerations. Many patients that came to the clinic had puzzling tropical skin infections and rashes. It seemed that everyone wanted eye glasses.

Every day before the clinic opened, the staff would get together and pray that God would lead them and show them how to properly diagnose each patient that they would meet that day. They prayed that there would be enough time in the day and adequate supplies to treat all of the hurting folks that came to the clinic.

When the clinic opened in the morning, there were typically many patients already waiting to be treated. Nurses provided triage as the support staff tried to keep order while the patients were waiting to see the medical team. The doctors had to have skilled Swahili interpreters working with them much of the time. After examining the patients, the doctor's diagnoses were written on an index card along with any medications that should be provided to that patient. Then the nurses would administer or distribute medications while instructing the patient through an interpreter regarding their use. Before the patient left the clinic, a treatment of some sort may have also been necessary.

The dentists felt that the clinic was fairly well equipped to handle their case load. However, those dentists had to practice without x-rays, one of their most important diagnostic tools. There were two dental chairs along with autoclaves for sterilizing instruments. In addition, there were boxes of dental supplies that had been previously shipped to Tanzania. The husband and wife dentist/periodontist team worked out of the two dental chairs in the back building. The second dentist set up his work area in the breezeway between medical and dental clinic buildings. He used a medical exam table for a patient chair. His practice offered a bit more primitive, but outdoorsy, dental experience.

The dentists saw 439 patients during their stay. Most of the patients that they examined and treated had never been to a dentist before in their lives. The care that the dentists provided was primarily problem and pain focused. A typical day in the clinic consisted mostly of pulling teeth, with a few fillings and cleanings conducted as well. If a patient had a toothache, the tooth was usually so severely decayed that it could not be restored. Extraction in most cases was the only option. Pulling of the teeth, instead of rebuilding them, began to wear on the dentists emotionally. In America the dentists tried to save every tooth. Eventually they became more comfortable with the fact that removals were in the patients' best interest. The extractions were relieving the patient's pain that some had suffered from for years.

The first four days of the health clinic were spent at the campus in Sakila.

Then the team was divided in half with one group traveling four kilometers by truck to a local public school where they set up a mobile clinic. The rest of the team stayed in Sakila to operate the clinic. This separation continued for two consecutive days. Then the first mobile team came back to the clinic and the other half went out to treat remote patients. The second group traveled four kilometers south to Kikatiti to set up a clinic in a local church.

The doctors were frequently uncertain of their diagnoses. They certainly were hampered by the lack of patient histories, labs and x-ray machines. The doctors also admitted to a limited knowledge of tropical medicine. Often all they could provide was some temporary relief from chronic symptoms. However, they always prayed with the people for their healing.

When the clinic first opened, three children arrived. An eleven year old girl brought her two younger siblings to be examined by the medical staff. The siblings that she brought with her looked like they may have been born a few years apart. The staff was shocked to find out that the younger children were really five year old twins with one boy being much smaller than the other. It was immediately obvious that the smaller child was malnourished and severely protein deficient. He had the classic symptoms of golden colored hair, which was brittle and falling out. His skin was also showing signs of the lack of protein. The medical personnel asked the older sister if her family had meat to eat. The reply was a simple "no." They then asked if the family fed the boy any eggs, beans or milk. To each item listed, the girl indicated that they had none of those foods.

A discussion was conducted among the staff on how to help the child. One member said that what would really help ease his malnourished condition was some powdered milk. That milk could be sent home with the children and it would provide at least some of the protein needed by the boy. The powdered milk would also keep over the long period of time that the boy would need to recover. However, no one knew of any available powdered milk and began to wonder if there was a store where that product was available for purchase.

Bishop Eliudi usually did not visit the clinic as he was very busy with his evangelism school and other projects. He left the treatment of the ill and injured to those who could do it the best. While the treatment of the malnourished youngster was being discussed, Eliudi happened to walk into the clinic to see how things were progressing.

Sami smiled at that good timing and asked Eliudi if he knew where the medical team could buy some powdered milk for the boy. He indicated that he had one 25 pound bag of it that someone had sent over from America in the last shipping container. Sami, realizing her good fortune and God's wonderful timing, asked Eliudi if she could have it to treat the sick child. Eliudi was more than happy to give the medical team the milk.

The bag was retrieved and given to the older sister with instructions on how to use the milk. After it was assured that the girl understood that each day the boy was to be given a glass of the milk, the staff prayed for the family. The prayer was needed as the medical staff knew that one glass of milk a day was not going to totally rectify the boy's condition. More protein was needed to allow him to fully recover.

On every trip back to Sakila, Sami has seen that boy in the village. He was growing normally and has not shown any more signs of malnutrition. God had provided the protein-rich milk for the child and then supplemented his daily intake with a more balanced diet. The boy is currently enrolled in school and is doing fine.

The medical team also examined a baby boy who was a couple months old and had been brought to the clinic by his mother. The team looked at the baby and saw that it was in critical respiratory distress and had a fever of 102. Not having the equipment to deal with the situation, the doctor conveyed to the mother that the baby needed to be taken to a hospital right away. He needed oxygen and antibiotics soon or he would die. To stabilize the baby, the nurses and support staff put together odds and ends of on-hand equipment that they could find to ease his constricted breathing condition.

While that emergency procedure was being accomplished, one of the staff informed Bishop Eliudi that a baby was in their care that would soon die if it was not transported to the hospital. Eliudi immediately summoned a driver and one of his vehicles to take the mother and baby to the public hospital in Arusha. The team doctor gave the driver the money required to have the baby admitted to the hospital. That money came from the ministry fund.

On the team's next visit to Sakila, the mother returned to the clinic and showed the medical staff the baby who was breathing just fine after his treatment. He was growing and in good health.

On the second day of the clinic, a nurse was trying to triage more than one hundred people who were waiting to be treated. As she was doing this very difficult task, a local woman interrupted her and just pleaded in English, "Please." The local woman and a woman standing next to her were holding identical twin girls. The mother said the twins were nine months old but neither looked big enough to be two months old. The little girls were very malnourished. One of the babies was even much smaller and weaker than the other. The interpreter told the nurse that the mother would soon have to choose which of the girls to save and which one she would let die. The mother was asking for help to save just one of the babies. As it happens, the triage nurse had twin children and could not imagine having to decide which one of her children would live while the other starved to death.

After one of the doctors examined the children, the team found some infant milk formula and a few feeding bottles which were stored obscured in a cardboard box in the east room. Then the team taught the mother how to use the formula. Bishop Eliudi's wife mixed up some bananas and rice water, which was fed to the babies as their first solid food. The nurse comforted the mother by telling her that she also had twin children and that she was very glad to have been able to help her through her difficult situation. When the mother and babies left for home, the team figured that for four dollars' worth of formula those twins had enough to eat for the next four months.

The Friday before the team left for home, the mother of the twins brought the babies back to show the team how well they were doing. She also had a piece of paper with her and told the interpreter that she wanted the nurse to write down the names of her twins. It was clear that the woman could not possibly pay for the medical care that she had received for her twins, but she could pray every day for the rest of her life for the nurse's twins. And that is exactly what she intended to do. An African mother who lives halfway around the planet is praying for the nurse's twins while the nurse is still praying to this day for that Tanzanian woman's twins.

Not all clinic visitors' stories have a happy ending. One day a mother brought her developmentally disabled child for screening. The boy was also afflicted with seizure disorders but had never seen a physician before. The clinic doctor explained to the mother that her child was special and his brain was different from other children. He explained that he would never be like the other kids in the village. The mother broke down and cried at the diagnosis. The last thing that the team did for the mother and boy was pray for them.

When a mobile clinic was set up, there was usually less patient control at the remote site than at the clinic in Sakila. With the large number of patients arriving at the mobile clinic, the local people were rightfully concerned that not all the individuals would be examined or treated in the length of time that the medical team was there.

Those mobile clinics were a time for extraordinary and sacrificial measures. At the end of the day with no more teeth to pull, the husband and wife dental team volunteered to wash the infected feet of two elderly people in Kikatiti. Instead of letting the patients put on their contaminated, tattered socks after the treatment, the dentists took their own shoes and socks off and gave their socks to the two seniors. On that same day, a nurse on the team gave her shoes to a very old woman who had none. That nurse had to return to Sakila in her socking feet while riding in the back of the truck.

One of the doctors on the team says of that first trip, "Although it was frustrating and tiring to be uncertain medically much of the time, it was encouraging to see God provide in so many small ways. Many times someone would say 'If we only had…' and someone else would answer 'I just saw some of that over there.' God also provided the team with stamina. We were protected from harm and no team member sustained injury despite working in poor light and in a lot of blood (particularly the dental team). The team was blessed by the interpreters and by the patients themselves. We witnessed such hope in the Africans; hope that they had because of their savior, Jesus Christ. The Africans told us that they would pray for us. We were awed by their faith."

In 2007, Sami Butler had another team working in Sakila. This time the team consisted of a surgeon, an ophthalmologist, three nurses, a pharmacy tech and a support person. This team would see over 1,000 patients during their stay.

Some of the medical conditions that were diagnosed were serious. One lady had a tumor on her tongue that looked cancerous and required surgery. There was also a woman with so much fluid in her abdomen that she looked nine months pregnant. She had no money to have the fluid drained or find out the cause. Through the ministry money fund the team paid to have both women admitted to the public hospital.

Seventeen year old twin girls from the local public primary school come to the clinic. Both of the girls wore thick eye glasses and indicated that they required new ones to see properly. They were trying to study for a very important, national school exam but could not see well enough to accomplish that. Through an interpreter, the staff was able to determine how much an eye exam in Arusha would cost for the two girls. Once the price was established, the girls were scheduled to be sent to Arusha where their eyes would be examined and new glasses purchased. The visiting medical team in Sakila paid for the exam and the new glasses from their ministry money. The money was given to the pastor of the girl's church to make sure that the funds went to the correct location. When the girls left to go to Arusha for the exam, they had tears streaming down their cheeks in deep gratitude for what was being done for them.

That year the team operated for the first week of their visit out of the clinic in Sakila. Through Bishop Eliudi's IEC contacts, an outreach clinic was planned in the village of Road Toll for three days. On each morning of the outreach, the medical supplies and equipment were loaded in the bed of the school truck. The team also found a place to ride in the back of the truck and was driven about 40 minutes away to the Masai village.

They held the clinic in an IEC church. Ropes and sheets were used to divide the church sanctuary into different medical areas. Even though the church building was the nicest building in the village, it had no electricity or running water. There was no glass in the barred windows and the eves under the tin roof were open. These conditions allowed the pigeons to fly into the church and through the treatment and exam areas.

The team treated about 400 people during the three day clinic in Road Toll. The last day of the visit was a very emotional experience. When the team arrived, there was a huge group waiting, with all of them wanting to be helped. Because it was their last day at the village, the team knew that they would not be able to see all of the waiting people. After the first fifty patients were admitted, the team closed the doors of the church and informed those left standing outside that they probably would not be seen that day. Instead of the crowd dispersing, it grew larger.

At mid-afternoon Sami Butler decided that the medical team should at least try to see any mothers with babies still outside and who had been waiting all day. Those mothers were picked out of the crowd and escorted into the church for examinations. A young Masai mother was admitted with a three month old infant that weighed only six pounds. The baby was septic and close to death. With their ministry funds completely used up, the medical team cleaned out their pockets of money and counted the total. They had exactly the 15,000 shillings that they needed to send the baby to the hospital and have it admitted. (15,000 shillings was worth about $10 US currency in that year.)

Those not being admitted to the church for treatment had to be warded off. The sick that were standing outside would point to open sores, crippled limbs, infected eyes and the like and begged to be treated.

As hard as this was on the medical staff to say no more exams, the pastor at the church had it worse. He had to explain to the waiting people, many of whom he knew, that they would not be seen on that final day of treatment. The medical team recognized the need, but there was only so much that they could do with the time and resources at hand.

The children of Tanzania seem to have a national past-time of asking Americans for "pipi," which is Swahili for candy. Since the team did not have any sweets, one of the nurses offered the kids of Road Toll hugs and held their hands. The children formed a circle around the nurse to receive their hugs. When she recognized one boy who had come around the circle for the fourth time, she knew that all of the kids had been hugged at least once. She reaffirmed to herself how valuable a simple touch can be.

Sami Butler had the medical teams returning to Sakila every two years. In 2009 the group consisted of eleven members. That team was made up of a doctor, a massage therapist, six nurses, a nursing student and two support staff. They would treat 1,350 Tanzanians during their visit.

Much of the same routine that was used before at the clinic was employed again. Lines would start forming at the clinic at 5 AM for the 8 AM opening. When the clinic opened up that year, cards with numbers printed on them were passed out to those waiting to determine the order in which the patients would be seen.

On the way back from the morning prayer service at the School of Evangelism, the medical workers noticed a middle-aged man who was already waiting in line. When the clinic opened, that middle aged gentleman was given a card with the number 12 on it. This card insured that the man would be examined early in the day.

Later in the morning a sick, young and pregnant woman arrived and received the number 64. Several people made room for her to sit down on the benches located outside the clinic. The crowd could tell she was not feeling well as she sat very still with her head held in her hands. After a few minutes, the middle-aged man got up from his bench and walked over to the ill, pregnant lady. He reached down and quietly exchanged his number for hers and then helped her to his former spot on the bench. She was one of the next people to be seen by the medical staff. The man, on the other hand, had to wait until late afternoon to be helped.

When the sun sets along the equator, there is very little twilight. As the sun drops below the western horizon, the immense sky rapidly becomes dark and filled with stars. After one busy day, the medical personnel were eating their evening meal and relaxing from their hectic schedule. The sun had set and a restful darkness had overtaken them. That night Bishop Eliudi was eating his evening meal with the medical staff.

Someone walked into the patio where the meal was being served and talked quietly to Eliudi. After listening to what was being said, Eliudi got the attention of the medical people and calmly said, "I guess your shift is not over yet. A fifteen year boy from the village was using a machete and has cut his right index finger to the bone. His family is requesting that someone treat his injury."

The medical team reassembled at the old clinic and examined the cut. The boy had not only cut the flesh on his finger, but also the tendons in the finger as well. Even with the overhead lights burning, the doctors and nurses wore head lamps to help illuminate the examination and treatment of the boy. Because the tendons in the finger are very small, they were hard to see and correct even under the best of conditions. The lack of lighting was going to be a serious problem to properly repair the finger. Before the procedure was started, the group prayed that God would guide their efforts and that He would allow them to see what they were doing. They also prayed that the finger would heal completely and work properly. The physician did what he could with the tendons and stitched the wounded finger closed. It was two years later that the staff saw the young man again and was delighted to see that he had full use of his finger.

That year the ministry money sent from the Montana church was used again to help sick and injured people. The team used those funds for numerous surgeries that were performed at hospitals in Arusha and Moshi. Abdominal tumors and eye cataracts were removed. One woman was treated at the hospital for a severe kidney infection. The medical staff prayed with all the patients that would receive treatments paid for from the ministry money fund. Then the patients were told that the money had come from God. They were also asked if they knew Jesus.

Even though the team shipped medical supplies to Sakila on the container in March, every day they would run out of one medication or another. A driver would be sent daily with ministry money to secure the needed medications and supplies. About the only thing that the team did not run out of were bars of soap, which were given to every person visiting the clinic.

The medical team stated that in many ways they received more blessings during the trip than they gave to the people being treated.

The Sami's fourth medical team left for Tanzania in the fall of 2011. That group was made up of a physician, two physician assistants, five nurses, a nursing student and a couple of support staff. Most of the team's visit was spent in villages in the area surrounding Sakila. That year was also a time of extreme drought in Eastern Africa. Since electricity is produced from generators located at various dam sites, electricity was almost non-existent due to the lack of water stored behind the dams.

On the first day of the 2011 visit, a lady came to the clinic with a tumor protruding from her back. It was causing her pain and making life miserable. When the tumor was examined, it was discovered to be the size of a tennis ball. The staff discussed their options on how to best proceed with the treatment. Superficial tumors had been successfully removed from patients before at the clinic, but it was a risky operation. Finally after some prayer, the staff referred the lady to the hospital and provided the funds required for the operation.

The day before the team was to leave to come home, that lady revisited the medical staff. She, like almost everyone else in Tanzania, had a cell phone. On that cell phone was a photograph of the tumor that was removed from her back. What had originally looked like a tennis ball sized tumor to the Sakila team was really as big as a frying pan under her skin. The medical team looked at her back and saw a large incision that was required to remove the tumor. They also examined the incision area to verify that it was healing properly. The woman was thrilled that the benign tumor was gone. The medical team was even more thrilled that they did not try to remove the tumor in the Sakila clinic. The operation would have escalated into something that they could not have handled properly. However if the tumor had been left in her body, it would have compromised some of her structural parts.

Even though the staff saw some patients at the Sakila clinic, most of the visit was spent at mobile clinics in IEC churches that were some distance from the school campus. The first village visited was 12 kilometers away in a place called Amani, which is Swahili for "peace." The road to Amani was bumpy and, because of the drought, very dusty.

Each clinic conducted was set up in the village church. Sometimes these churches had only dirt floors. Sheets were again hung on ropes to segregate the medical areas within the church. There was no shelving to spread out the medical supplies, so the team worked out of cardboard boxes. When all was ready and the indispensable interpreters were standing by, the doors to the church were opened to admit the first patients. The teamed worked hard and busily all day long until after the last patient was allowed in.

At times the medical team felt dissatisfied as patients with chronic aches and pains were given little more than a few Tylenol pills. That was a remedy that may work for a few hours at the most, but it was the best that the team could do. An old woman waited six hours to be told that her hand injury could not be fixed. However there were also meaningful and helpful outcomes. A few women patients who were suffering from goiters were supplied with enough medicine to last them a year. In one day, $1,000 was spent referring patients to Arusha to get surgery, dental work or specialty consultations.

The pastor and the women of the IEC church served the team lunch. It consisted of watermelon and what looked like fried chicken legs. Along with those items, rice with a stew of potatoes and beef or goat was also served. The pastors provided the team with soda pop, a luxury in Tanzania. With no refrigeration, the pop was warm and awfully sweet. Even with the need to eat, it was awkward to stop the flow of patients through the mobile clinic. Patients had been waiting since before sunup to be seen. Some of the team felt guilty eating while those waiting in line had nothing to eat.

In the afternoon, an 85 year old Masai woman with acute pneumonia was brought into the sanctuary. She had been carried to the front of the line after someone found her lying in the dust and hot sunshine near the side of the road close to the church. Since she did not speak Swahili, the medical team needed two translators to communicate with the woman. The physician assistant examined her and was terrified that she would not be able to do enough to heal the elderly woman. After the lady was treated and prayed for, the staff insured that someone would see her safely home.

When the team was finished for the day, they started to dump out the small tubs of wash water that was used to cleanse their hands. There was probably one quart of dirty water per tub. The local pastor came running and pleaded with the team to put the water into a big plastic storage tank. The drought was so severe that the village wanted to reuse the team's dirty water.

At the end of each day during their visit that year, it was time to climb into the truck, ride back to Sakila, unload and repack the boxes for the next day. The medical team was tired, dirt-caked and ready to go to sleep. Because of the drought and lack of electricity, the team got to shower only once every three days. That shower consisted of a cold rinse off for a few seconds, which was just enough to jolt them awake and wash off some of the grime. On the next day they may be off to a new village or to treat the orphans in Arusha.

At the end of one long day of seeing patients, one of the interpreters said to the medical team, "I do not know if you realize how powerful your medical ministry is. Today in this village, you have treated church members and other Christians. You have also treated non-Christians and Muslims. And you treated them all the same. The villagers look at you and see Jesus. You are a very powerful example of the Christian faith to them."

CHAPTER 15:

GOD IS THE BUILDER OF EVERYTHING

(Hebrews 3:4)

Marion and Loretta Sluys of Poulsbo, WA have always been a mission-orientated couple. In their early years they spent many months working in the mission field in the South Pacific, engaged in many projects on the islands of Western Samoa and Tonga. Marion was part of a team that built a church on an island near Guadalcanal. The couple has also been to Mexico to assist with a medical mission there.

In 1989 they were invited to a dinner party on Bainbridge Island where Bishop Eliudi spoke. Marion and Loretta were impressed with this Tanzanian and his vision for winning souls. After Eliudi addressed their home church, they decided to support the fledging ministry. However, Marion had heard that Africa was a dark hole to invest his funds. A person could spend a lot of money there and expect little or no return.

In 1990 seventeen members of Gateway Fellowship and a few other near-by churches went to Sakila to build a house for the evangelism school teachers and to closely examine the mission operations there. The completed house was to be called the Washington House because the volunteers who built it were from Washington State. This was the group that Bob Smith joined for his first trip to Africa.

Since the group was too big for Eliudi's Land Rover, the Washingtonians were transported from the Kilimanjaro Airport to Sakila in a bus. When they arrived at the school campus, all the students were gathered alongside the road, singing and dancing with music and waving flowers to welcome their guests. (The workers would also be sent home in the same manner.)

After their arrival, the builders found the conditions there close to primitive. Guards walked around the fourteen acre campus at night to protect the property from looters. Since there was no electricity at the time, there was no running water. The church members from Washington State slept in a single-room building and used sleeping bags laid on mattresses placed on the cement floor for beds. There was a partition dividing the inside of the building in half. The three ladies who went along on the trip slept on one side of the partition and the 14 men on the other side. Since sleeping was uncomfortable and difficult, many of the volunteers told stories or discussed building plans into the small hours of the night, which tended to keep the others awake.

The Washington House was built using solid, preformed cement blocks which were mortared together up to a level where the lintels (or top) of the windows would be. Next a ten-inch high, cement header was to be poured on top of the blocks. This header is used to reinforce and unite the walls of the structure. Wooden boards are used as a form, which is placed around the top of the blocks and in which the cement would be poured. To aid in this construction, a gas powered concrete mixer had been shipped over to Sakila to thoroughly blend the cement ingredients. As they reviewed the task ahead, the group knew that they were in for a long day of cement mixing and pouring.

When Eliudi discovered what the visitors had planned for that day's activities, he told the group that he would have his school students do the cement work instead. Sixty students, men and women, gathered at the construction site and blended the gravel, sand and dry cement mix using hand tools to form a five foot high cone on the ground. The top of the little mountain was cratered out before pouring water into the depression. A few students stood on the cone and slurried the water and mix together. The wet cement was then passed on to other students in large dish-shaped pans. The wet mix was carried to additional students standing on ladders or staging positioned at the top of the walls where the mix was poured into the form. Within an hour and half, the cement was all poured allowing the construction of the remaining portion of the walls and a roof to continue. The mechanical cement mixer had not been needed.

However, a number of the Bible students arrived at the clinic the next day complaining of sore chest muscles. The students were assured that they did not have anything seriously wrong with them and were simply suffering from the previous day's strenuous work.

When the walls were completed, stucco was applied to the outside of the structure. The students would scoop the wet stucco mix with a pointed trowel and flick it at the wall where it would stick to the concrete blocks. After the block wall was thoroughly coated, the students smoothed the applied mix with a board or a flat trowel.

Marion tried to duplicate the student's flicking efforts with his trowel. No matter how hard he tried, he could not throw the stucco at the wall in the correct manner to where it would stick. Even after the students showed him how to do it over again, Marion still could not make the stucco adhere to the wall. His efforts brought much laughter to the students and to Marion.

After many tries, Marion finally mastered the art of throwing the stucco and having it adhere to the wall. A sore wrist confirmed his newly acquired talent. However, his wife, Loretta, wondered what they were going to do with all the stucco that had landed in the dirt during Marion's apprenticeship.

After returning to Poulsbo with a favorable report about the International Evangelism Centre, Marion thought that he could further help the mission campus by shipping cooking oil to Africa for the school cooks to use. The goat fat that the chefs were using to prepare the food was not sanitary enough to ensure healthy meals. For the next several years the Sluys would send fifteen 55 gallon drums of cooking oil. Cooks employed a motor-oil hand pump to draw the oil out of the drums. Once the drums were empty, the Sakila villagers would use the drums for various purposes such as staging foundations.

Rice is one of the mainstays of the African diet. But, the rice available in Tanzania has little white rocks mixed in with the rice, which are difficult to see and very damaging to teeth. To protect their teeth, the Africans would spread the rice out and try to go through it thoroughly to winnow out as many of the rocks as possible. Marion and fellow church member, Leroy Snyder, came up with the idea of shipping American-grown rice, which has no rocks in it, each year to the school. The first year's shipment consisted of six tons of bagged rice. By 2012 that amount had grown to 15 tons in order to also supply some rice for primary and secondary school functions.

In years past, five pallets of rice were temporarily deposited in the lobby of Gateway Fellowship. Between church services, those involved with the Sakila mission would take donations from church members to help defray the costs of shipping the rice to Africa. With each donation given, the person or family could mark on the bag of rice their name and a message. This message could be a greeting or a Bible verse. Then the rice was loaded into a shipping container and sent to Tanzania. When each bag of rice was opened in Sakila, the school staff would pray a blessing for each person whose name appeared on the bag.

The Sluys went back to Sakila in 1993 and built another structure constructed of two forty-foot metal shipping containers. This building was also to be used as sleeping quarters for the teachers. A forty by forty foot concrete slab was poured with the containers placed opposite each other on the dried cement. Truss beams were built spanning the containers and the area between them to support a roof. Then two walls were installed in each container to make three rooms. When the construction was done, the teachers liked the building so much that they decided to use it as an office instead of a dormitory. That structure became known as Washington Square.

One of the empty cooking oil barrels came in handy for the construction crew in 1993. Since there was no automatic way to heat water at the campus, one of the barrels was placed on three cement blocks and filled with water from one of Bruce Crower's wells. The space under the barrel was stacked with wood which was lit on fire and kept burning all day. This arrangement provided hot water for the group's evening showers.

The heated water was poured in sun shower bags which were hung high enough to allow gravity to feed the water to the shower head. The plastic bags insured that each person would have three gallons of water to complete their shower. (Sun shower bags are generally an item that wilderness hikers use to bathe with. The bags are normally filled with water in the morning, allowing the sun to heat the water during the day.)

A small three walled structure was built against a building in Sakila for the ladies to shower in. Since it afforded privacy, the men also used the facility after the women's showers were finished. The group was surprised at how clean they could get by just using half of the contents of the sun shower bags. The fresh water supply was still at a premium in Sakila.

To provide sanitary facilities for the Americans, squat-and-go toilets were built. Usually toilets in Africa are not like the ones normally found in the United States. The western toilet bowl and seat would be too difficult to keep clean and sanitized in a village in Africa. Without running water, they would also be un-flushable. In Tanzania a pit was dug in the ground and covered over with a cement slab which had a small opening in it over the pit. Walls and a roof were constructed around the openings in the cement slab. Scuff marks or a raised area on the floor indicated where a person's feet were to be placed so that when a person squatted, they would have their rear correctly placed over the opening in the floor. When using the toilet in the dark, raised foot pads were more than convenient. The facility that the villagers made for the Americans was a six holer which provided some much needed privacy. The squat-and-goes did have an inconvenience that the westerners soon discovered. As they squatted, items placed in their jean pockets could slide out and possibly drop down the hole in the cement slab.

During their first two trips to Sakila, the day began very early. The evangelism students met at the school building for prayer around four o'clock in the morning. The American workers were awakened in the early morning to the pleasing sound of praying. The beautiful resonance of praise and worship was like a wind of voices rolling through the African valley.

The Americans would often join the prayer meeting before the sun rose. Since there was no electricity for lights, the time of prayer was conducted in the dark. The Americans would arrive at the school room and fumble around to find a place to stand in the pre-dawn blackness. Since it was hard to see Africans in the dark, the workers did not know who it was that they had inadvertently bumped into or where they should shuffle off to next. With the rising sun, there were a mixture of Meru, Swahili, English and Holy Spirit languages praising God. Eliudi would end the meeting with a prayer before everyone would go to breakfast.

The only light that was present for the dark walk to the church was provided by flashlights that the Americans had brought with them from home. However, they soon discovered that even if it was pitch black out, the well-used trails could be seen.

Except for the hand-held flashlights, evening religious services were also conducted without lights. The presence of God was felt by the westerners when in the darkness; the students would sing heart-felt songs of praise.

The heavenly voices verbally lit up the dark African night.

On some Sundays Eliudi would take the Americans out into the country-side to a different village to conduct a church service. As there were no buildings in the villages which were big enough to accommodate everyone in attendance, those services were held outside. During these services, Loretta was always amazed at how freely the Africans worshipped God. When the offering was taken, not all that was given was money. There might be a chicken, some eggs, or a small bag of rice in the collection plate. The people gave back to God from what they had.

After some of the church services, the village would honor the visiting workers by killing and cooking a goat. The various churches roasted the goat for different lengths of time resulting in some meat that was prepared well done. Usually however, the goat meat was simply rare. Unfortunately the goat carcass was not over the cooking fire long enough before it was retrieved, carved and served. That resulted in the meat being quite under cooked when it was served to the guests.

Most westerners felt that the goat was not cooked long enough for them to enjoy. However, protocol dictates that everyone in attendance must eat a piece of meat. To avoid eating more of the usually very rare meat, the guests could "pass-the-privilege-on" to the villagers. Since the villagers seldom have meat to eat, the visitors would honor the tradition and eat a small portion of the goat indicating that they loved it. Next they would say that they had had enough to eat and preferred that the villagers take their deserved share of the goat.

When Loretta thinks back on her experiences in Tanzania she says, "Life is simpler over there. The people welcome you with open arms. There is a lot of hand shaking and greeting. You do not always understand the language but you can see the warmth of their heart. A lady who lived in Sakila was at an outdoor get-together one evening and gave me a ring. It was not a valuable piece of jewelry, but it was probably all she had. The ring was a gift from her heart. It is wonderful to be around people who accept you as you are and love you anyway."

Loretta continues, "The work that is happening in Sakila is really amazing and is helping those wonderful people. And all this came about by a vision that a man named Eliudi received from God. You can't help but want to support and progress the mission there."

CHAPTER 16:

WHOEVER WELCOMES A LITTLE CHILD
(Matthew 18:5)

Since Gene and Lorraine Anderson of Port Orchard, WA were empty nesters in 2002, they asked God what He had for them to accomplish next. Their children were out of the house, the last elderly parent had passed on and Gene and Lorraine were retired. For them it was time to serve God in a new way. Within two weeks of asking God for direction, they received it.

Four years before in 1998 when Godwin and his wife, Kim, were living in Sakila, the idea of establishing a preschool there came to them. They saw younger kids who were out playing in the village but who should have been learning in a structured school environment. A major reason why the local kids were not in school was that the nearest public school was over-crowded. There were nearly one hundred preschool students with just one teacher.

As a result, Godwin and Kim decided to inaugurate a preschool of their own. To conduct and house the preschool, Godwin and Kim utilized an old chicken coop near the evangelism school. As Tanzanian preschools did not need any government certification, the preschool was operated as the local community desired. Immediately after the school started, there were one hundred students enrolled. Godwin paid some of the mothers of the village to teach. Even though their salary was just $1.50 a month, the mothers were happy to do it. Among the items that they taught the kids was to sing, write the alphabet and numbers, and speak a few English words. More importantly, the preschool got the children's minds prepared for the public school's kindergarten. In 2002 Providence Vineyard Christian Fellowship in Stayton, Oregon donated some money to construct a building for the preschool on the School of Evangelism campus in order to relocate the kids from the chicken coop.

Soon the kids were absorbing knowledge at a prodigious rate. When those youngsters went to public school, their learning skills were so far beyond the other kids that they started creating problems. The main problem was that the Sakila kids needed to be advanced to higher grade levels; and the school administrators and teachers were not sure what to do about that. It then became obvious to Godwin and Kim that there was a need for a private kindergarten in Sakila to continue the education which the kids were receiving at the preschool. At that point, the mothers who were hired to teach at the preschool started praying to God for a new primary school to be built.

After two trips to Sakila, Marion and Loretta Sluys did not return to Tanzania until 2002. Their plan was to take another large group over to the evangelism school to build showers and a sewer system to handle the run-off. Twelve new squat-and-go toilets were planned to be built as well. However, individuals were not volunteering for the trip to Africa as they had in the past. Marion felt that he would need to get more aggressive in his recruiting endeavors.

One Sunday after church at Gateway Fellowship in Poulsbo, WA, Marion was in the parking lot delivering an antique milk can to Lorraine and Gene Anderson which they had requested from him. At that time, Marion asked them if they would like to go to Africa and help build some new showers at a school. Gene thought for just a second or two and said that he would love to go. Lorraine had completely different thoughts. She said, "I will send money over but I do not have the manual skills to go to Africa to build things."

Since this was during one of Eliudi's visits to the United States, he overheard Lorraine's reason for not wanting to go to Sakila. Bishop Eliudi chuckled and said to Lorraine that she did not have to help with the construction but could play with the children. He explained that his son Godwin had established an impromptu preschool for the small children of the school staff and for some of the local families. Lorraine could tag along with the builders and help out with those little kids. She would be used in Sakila to keep the young kids occupied during the day by telling them some Bible stories. Since that assignment won Lorraine over, the Andersons were booked on the next trip to Sakila.

On the flight over, Loretta told Lorraine about the squat-and-go toilet facilities present on the school campus. After arrival in Sakila, Lorraine was delighted to discover that the guest rooms which Eliudi had built for his western visitors had sit-down toilets and running water.

Later she discovered that standing water anywhere in Tanzania invited little green frogs to congregate. Those frogs thought that toilet bowls made excellent swimming pools. Even after they were flushed down the drain, the frogs would somehow swim back up the piping and into the bowl. Those frogs caused more than a little consternation to the visitors whenever they were sitting on the toilet seats.

With the advent of running water, the sun shower bags were no longer used. However with the continuing shortage of rain, personal showers were still limited to a short duration.

Since the school leaders in Sakila knew what was planned to be built by the Americans, they had constructed a large portion of the shower and toilet facilities before the volunteers arrived. As a result, what remained of the building project did not take long for the Americans to complete. In their free time, the ladies of the group fell in love with the pre-school children of Sakila.

After the volunteers returned to the United States, Bishop Eliudi sent Gene and Lorraine a message asking them to start a sponsorship program for the local school-aged children. While he was in America, Eliudi had learned about sponsorship programs where westerners would pay for a student to go to school in the student's home country.

Before they committed themselves to organizing a sponsorship program, Gene and Lorraine knew it would be an immense undertaking. When they asked their church pastor if he would support them in the endeavor, Pastor Pearson of Gateway Fellowship gave them his blessing with one piece of advice. Since the African and American cultures were so different, he thought that they should use Eliudi's son Godwin as a go-between to sort out the different expectations of a sponsorship program. (Godwin and his family had returned to the United States and were living near Poulsbo at the time.) With that assurance and advice, the Sakila Sponsorship Program

(SSP) was born.

The first order of business that the Andersons accomplished was to mail out sponsorship information to all of their friends and relatives on their Christmas card list. In the mailings, they stated that this would be the first and last time their acquaintances would hear about the program if they chose not to sponsor a child. From those mailings, they received only one sponsorship application. After that, Gene and Lorraine decided it was time to drastically expand their sponsorship efforts.

In January of 2003, the first sponsorship presentation at Gateway Fellowship was given. In front of the Poulsbo congregation, the Andersons explained that sponsors were needed to pay for the students' education while they attended school in Tanzania. The original sponsorship was set at $20 a month. That amount of money would pay for the teacher's salary plus buy necessary supplies and a school uniform for each student. On the first day of the appeal, people lined up to support a child or to simply give a donation. The congregation sponsored 60 of the 80 kindergarten students on that day!

During the following years, it was a bit harder to secure sponsors as the members of Gateway Fellowship were already sponsoring a majority of students. This led the Andersons, with the help of Marion and Loretta Sluys, to visit different churches in Western Washington and out of state to ask their members if they would sponsor some of the children.

Each year the necessary task of enlisting enough sponsors for the new children was conducted. Gene talked to Rotary, Kiwanis and any other organization that would listen to him in order to convince people to sponsor students. Because of God's blessings, enough sponsors have continued to sign up to meet the expenses of the program.

After the kindergarten children finished one year of schooling, they became first graders. The Andersons were in a quandary about what to do next. To talk things over, they called Godwin to meet them and the Sluys the following day at noon at Starbucks in Poulsbo. Godwin indicated that he would be there to meet with them.

However, on that day Godwin realized that he would not be able to attend the Sluys and Anderson's meeting because of a previously scheduled engagement in Seattle. As a result, he emailed the Andersons and the Sluys to inform them that he would be unable to meet with them. Before Godwin left his office in Port Gamble, he had a package that needed to be mailed. There was a mailing service in his building, but for some reason he decided to drive a little out of his way to Poulsbo to ship the package before catching the ferry to Seattle. After driving to Poulsbo, parking and mailing the package, he walked out of the mailing service to find Gene, Lorraine, Marion and Loretta waiting for him beside his car. From Starbucks which is near the UPS store, they had seen Godwin park his car before mailing the package. Since Godwin was late for their meeting, they went to his car to welcome him to the meeting.

Godwin quizzed them, "What are you folks doing here? Didn't you get my email that stated I could not attend your meeting?" Both the Sluys and the Andersons indicated that they had not.

Godwin saw on their faces that they thought that their meeting was very important. As a result, he phoned the people he was to meet in Seattle and told them that something had occurred to cause him to miss their appointment. (This important conference, that would be crucial for the children of Sakila, was only convened through the timely direction of God.)

Seated in Starbucks, the Andersons asked Godwin what the Sakila Sponsorship Program should do for the students entering the first grade. Godwin suggested that the first graders could be sent to public school with the financial support contributed to the child's parents or guardian. Godwin also wanted an at-school meal program, but he said that he could not fathom how he could combine the public school attendance with the distribution of food for the sponsored children. At the same time, the Andersons and Sluys were not convinced that the sponsored children would get a good education at the public schools.

Marion then asked Godwin what he would need to do to assure that the children would get the best education. Godwin said that they would require property on which to build their own primary school and obtain a government certification for that school. Marion then indicated that he had some money which he said he would donate and which he thought would go a long way towards paying for the land. He asked Gene if he could donate some funding as well. Gene and Lorraine talked it over between themselves for a few minutes and contributed enough money that they believed would be necessary to complete the purchase of the land.

With that total established, they specified to Godwin what that amount was. Marion then looked at Godwin and requested that he ask his father to look for some property to buy. Marion thought, "If this school was God's plan, He would open the appropriate doors."

Godwin called his father in Sakila to inform him of the proposal and how much funding was available for the purchase of the land. Bishop Eliudi knew that buying land in Tanzania was very difficult, if not impossible, due to the existing property laws. Those laws stated that if a person wanted to purchase land in Tanzania and someone was already living on that land, the buyer could not take possession of the land until the selling family was relocated to a comparable property and house. Before the deal was completed, the new house and land had to meet the seller's approval.

It was just three days later that Eliudi called Godwin and said that he was amazed at what had transpired; he had located land near Sakila for the primary school. He had acquired from four families a verbal sale agreement of 6.5 acres that happened to be just a mile from the IEC campus. Replacement land had already been found for the displaced families to move to. When the funds were transferred to Tanzania, the land was purchased and became a satellite of the IEC campus. Everyone involved knew that God had easily opened that door! It was then time to start a school building project on the parcel of land.

In January 2004 another appeal was made at Gateway Fellowship for student sponsors. On that Sunday, the church also took a benevolence offering that was to be used to help needy families and individuals in the Poulsbo area.

It seems that during the church service a lady was going to drop a check into the benevolence offering collection plate, but somehow the plate was not passed down her row in the balcony. The lady then decided that after the service, she would look for Lorraine and hand the check to her instead.

Between services the Andersons and Sluys were standing by ready to enroll people for Sakila sponsorships. The woman from the balcony found Loretta Sluys who introduced her to Lorraine and explained that she had a check for the school. It was written for $8,700. Lorraine looked in amazement at the sum and exclaimed, "Do you know what this money will build in Tanzania?" Indeed, that donation built the first primary school building in Sakila. The building would have five classrooms and a primary school office, thanks to the generous donation.

Not fifteen minutes later another lady approached Lorraine with another donation. After church, that woman and her husband were driving home. The lady told her husband that she had to go back to the church right away to give a $20 donation to the Tanzanian school project. (Lorraine could only imagine what her husband thought of that request.) The husband was a little reluctant to return to the church as he felt that $20 probably would not make that much of a difference to the overall sponsorship program. However, back at the church the lady handed Lorraine the twenty dollar bill and said, "The Lord wants me to give this to you." Lorraine clearly realized that God was telling her that she should not focus on the donated amount, but on the giver's obedience to Him. If the lady had handed that cash to anyone else, Lorraine felt that she may have never learned that lesson. Lorraine never saw the woman again.

The donations that were obtained started the construction of what would be known as the Sluys/Anderson Primary School in Sakila. Since the land was somewhat swampy it had to be partially drained in order to build on it. The first structure erected was the long building with five classrooms situated end to end and the office. Then at 90 degrees to that building Marion Sluys had some buildings constructed that contained two classrooms each. Additional classrooms were built with funds from the Sakila Sponsorship Program. There are 16 classrooms at the primary school today.

Later, the Sluys also erected a building that would house a computer lab. Lisa Zempel was a teacher at a public junior high school in Gillette, WY whose donations supplied the lab with 40 new computers. She had visited Sakila and came home with a burden for the students at the Sluys/Anderson School. Lisa spoke to the principal at the public school where she taught in Gillette and asked if she and her students could adopt the computer lab as their class project. The principal gave his consent for her to do what she could for the school in Tanzania. Through many fund raising events, the public school students gathered $22,225 to buy the needed computers. That year when the shipping containers destined for Sakila were loaded in Poulsbo, WA, the Wyoming school sent Ms. Zempel, another teacher and five students to load those computers into the containers. The school paid the group's air fare, lodging and meals.

The Sluys/Anderson School administration building was funded by the

Lighthouse Christian Church of Port Angeles, WA. Ann Connolly of Poulsbo paid for the construction of a cook house on the primary school site to serve as a shelter for the cooks as they prepared meals for the students.

Of course, one of the first necessities was an adequate supply of good clean water. Trusty Matheson was soon on the job and drilled two wells near the primary school. The electrical lines that the government had promised had finally arrived before the school construction began. To be sure, electrical power was not constantly flowing through the wires, but the lines had arrived. Large above-ground tanks were purchased and connected to the wells with pipe. When the power was on, the well pump filled the storage tanks with water that would be available during times when the electricity was not energizing the pump. The water in the tanks was gravity fed via piping to valves near the ground.

Electricity in Tanzania is almost solely generated from hydro-electric sources. During April through June, the rains are more common. When the dams have backed up enough water during those months, electricity comes over the utility wires almost constantly. After the dryer months of August and September as the water supply dries up, power from the dams is intermittent. In October and November, electrical power may be provided only two or three hours a day.

Once the school buildings were finished, it was time to populate the school with students. An announcement was circulated around Sakila that applications were being taken from parents or guardians who wanted their children to attend the private school. The first year there were 360 applications summited to Godwin whose job it would be to pick the actual students. Because there were only 80 openings available that year, many disappointed parents and guardians were turned away. From the beginning, the school accepted students regardless of their religion or place in life. Teachers for the school were hired from throughout the northern Tanzania and southern Kenya area.

The last requirement that had to be completed for the school to officially start was the awarding of the government certification. Normally this process takes two to three years to complete. Some schools in Tanzania have actually taken as long as ten years to be presented with the certification. But thanks to the Lord, the primary school in Sakila required just two months to gain approval.

The story of how the certification came so quickly was another door being opened by God. While visiting the School of Evangelism in Sakila on an unrelated matter, the Tanzanian Minister of Education was conferring with Bishop Eliudi. Before the Minister left Sakila, Eliudi happened to mention to the gentleman that they were starting a primary school near the school campus. Eliudi verbally wondered if the Minister might help them speed the certification forms through the government bureaucracy. The Minister of Education said, "Fill out the paper work and bring it directly to my office. I will see that the certification is promptly taken care of and approved." The two months that it took to acquire the certification was mostly taken up by Eliudi and Godwin filling out the forms.

When Bishop Eliudi thinks back to the beginning of the primary school, he usually laughs a little. He said that a group of people from Washington State were coming to the IEC campus to build showers and a sewer system. Before anyone knew what had happened, God had used those people to start a primary school for the children near Sakila. In rapid succession, land was purchased, classrooms built, teachers hired and students were being taught in a God-centered environment. With God's direction and leading through the Sakila Sponsorship Program, the school was being sustained and growing.

CHAPTER 17:

LET THE LITTLE CHILDREN COME UNTO ME
(Luke 18:16)

At times there are nearly 600 students at the Sluys/Anderson Primary School. The school encompasses kindergarten and first through seventh grades. Kindergarteners receive porridge in the morning and are sent home at noon. The rest of the students receive a noon-time meal. For the younger kids, a morning meal is also served. For really needy children, food is also being offered before the children go home in the evening. When necessary, medical care is also provided for the students.

Because uniforms are a Tanzanian requirement, the program purchased one every year for each student at the elementary school for nearly a decade. Now the families are required to buy the student's uniform. Having the parents buy the uniform saves SSP funding and gives the family a sense of ownership for their child's education. If the family is too poor to acquire a uniform, SSP still supplies for that need.

Established educational standards are firmly maintained at the school. If a student does not measure up to standards of their grade, they are not promoted to the next grade. Discipline is also strictly enforced.

In Tanzania each student is tested by the government at the end of the fourth and seventh grades. If the student in a government school does not pass that fourth grade national test, the student cannot advance to fifth grade until that test is satisfactorily passed. If a student fails the seventh grade national exam, he or she is removed from school and never allowed to continue on to secondary school. That seventh grade evaluation test cannot be re-taken and the score of that one test stays with the student for the rest of his or her life. It is important to note that the government of Tanzania administers those evaluation tests.

The students at the Sluys/Anderson School are tested along with the rest of the students in the country. At this time every Sluys/Anderson student who has taken the national seventh grade test has passed it except one. That fact places the school at the top of all the schools in the country. (The one student who failed the seventh grade exam did so by a miniscule margin. Since this is a private school, that student was allowed to continue on to the secondary school and is doing quite well.)

The Tanzanian education officials have expressed a desire to come to Sakila and see why the children there have scored so well. Loretta Sluys says, "The reason for the success at the school is that the teachers are dedicated to the students. They will tutor the students after school and on weekends as required. They will also tutor the student during the months of the year when the school is closed. The teachers firmly believe in the school and its mission. Plus, most parents are totally supportive of the education that their youngsters are receiving."

Another reason for the success of the school is that primary grade school teachers usually have no more than 40 students in their class. When 80 students are admitted to the school, the students are divided into two classes. As stated before, the Tanzanian public schools can have as many as 100 students or more in a class.

In the early days of the school, Bishop Eliudi had the parents or guardians of each student come to the Sakila campus on the first Monday of every month. First order of business on those Mondays was that all the parents or guardians pray for the school and the sponsors who were putting their children through school. The rest of the parents' day was spent working around the campus completing general projects. There has never been any objection about the Bible being taught or Christian prayer being a part of the daily routine.

The reader might ask, "What does the local public school think of the Sluys/Anderson Primary School?" To answer that it should be noted that the principal and one of the teachers at the near-by public school send their children to the Sluys/Anderson School. Because of the nutrition programs at the primary schools, the public school teachers remark that the SSP students look healthier than most of the public school kids. The SSP school has also set an example for the public school which has cleaned up their grounds and buildings to make it more inviting for children to play and learn there. When the primary school was built, the public school did not have electricity or a clean water supply.

The Sluys/Anderson School thrived over the years and before a lot of people noticed, the students were about ready to graduate from seventh grade. "Where are our kids to go to continue their education?" the parents asked. The logical answer was that a secondary and a high school should be built to further their education. (It should be noted that Tanzanian primary schools only conduct classes through the seventh grade. After the seventh grade, the students advance directly to the secondary school level. The standard secondary school has a duration of four years. After that period of time, a "high school" is operated for two more years. The high school teaches a pre-college curriculum.)

To understand how God brought the secondary school into existence, the reader has to travel back a number years. Sometime before in Tanzania, a Muslim individual had bought land a quarter of a mile north of where the primary school property would be with the intention of building a mosque. The School of Evangelism staff felt apprehensive at the thought of such a building being constructed near their village. They and the evangelism school students prayed against the mosque project. Fortunately because of a "lack of funding," that mosque was never built.

The Muslim man then sold the property to another man who was thinking that the property would be a good investment. It was a nice ten-acre piece of property with banana trees and coffee plants. The land had much better drainage than the nearby land that the primary school sat on. However, the man's children tried to talk their father out of buying the land as it was too far away from their homes. Discouraged, the man let the land sit idle for a long time. In fact, that land sat idle for a total of 34 years with no one building on it. It seems that God had his own plans for the property.

In 2008 Bishop Eliudi received a request from his supporters in Washington State to start a search for suitable land on which to build a secondary school. He started looking around for a site while quizzing land owners of their possible intent to sell. The man who owned the property near the primary school saw this as his golden chance to divest himself of land that he could not use and that his family did not want. The owner of the property appraised the land at $50,000. (Land value in the Sakila area had increased considerably since Eliudi had bought the one hundred acre farm for the School of Evangelism.)

As the total funding of the secondary school property had not yet been acquired, another miracle was about to come from God. A sum of $6,000 was all that SSP had on hand for purchasing the secondary school property. Gene and Lorraine suggested to Eliudi that he could use that money as a down payment. However, down payments are never used in the Tanzanian culture to secure property. A land buyer paid the full amount or he did not purchase the land. But surprisingly after discussing the financial situation, the owner was more than happy to sell the property to Bishop Eliudi starting with a $6,000 down payment and promptly signed over the deed to the land.

Obviously, the funding for the rest of the property had to be quickly secured from SSP supporters to finish paying off the remaining cost of the land. Even though the largest donation received was $1,000, the remaining $44,000 was raised in just thirteen months.

That single $1,000 gift came completely unexpected. The Andersons check their email for the last time late in the evening. One night they noticed that in their in-box there was a $1,000 gift for SSP and it was from someone in California that they had never heard of before. Lorraine sent them a message, "Thank you for your generous donation. Just how did you learn of our organization?" The returned story related that Marion and Loretta Sluys were vacationing in Hawaii and relaxing beside the swimming pool one day. Suddenly, Loretta exclaimed to Marion that she believed that a man in the pool was drowning. Marion, who was 75 years old at the time, leaped into the pool and saved the man's life. In gratitude for the timely rescue, the man sent the $1,000 donation to the Sakila Sponsorship Program. That money was applied to the secondary school property fund.

With property in hand, the first buildings were erected. Teachers and a headmaster were hired for the new school which was named the Sakila Hebron Secondary School. (Sakila is located in an area in Tanzania known as Hebron.) Those students graduating from the primary school began attending classes at the new secondary school in 2010.

Per Tanzanian law, the pre-college, high school students must be housed as boarding students at a site near or on the school grounds. In 2012 the first 49 live-in students arrived at the Sakila Hebron School from other unsuccessful private schools in Tanzania. At this time new multi-story dormitories are being constructed to house those boarding students. Until those units are built, the boarding students are living in various buildings around the International Evangelism Centre and primary school campus.

The secondary school received its certification in less than one short year. The standard certification documentation informs the school's operators of the maximum number of students that can be enrolled in each grade per year. Normally that number is established at 80 to 85 students per class. The Tanzanian government felt so confident in the Sakila educational program that the certificate states that Hebron can have as many as 400 students in each class!

So far, the construction of all of the Hebron's school buildings has been funded. One family at Gateway Fellowship paid for all of the secondary classrooms to be erected. People who have flown to Tanzania to work at the IEC mission campus are the individuals who are paying for those buildings. Eliudi says, "Some people say that instead of visitors paying to fly to Sakila, that air fare money should just be donated to the mission in order to help the people. However, if a person comes to Sakila, he or she will catch the mission vision because they can see it, feel it and sense it. That is more helpful to me than all the monetary donations I could ever receive."

When western visitors are in Africa talking to the Sakila Hebron headmaster, the headmaster often mentions that the students at the high school will need a university after they graduate. Those supporters believe that if God wants a university in Sakila, doors will be opened and it will happen.

When Gene Anderson looks back to the beginning of the Sakila Sponsorship Program, he says, "The entire process has been a miracle. What is really amazing is that God is using us for His student sponsorship program. We are not professional school organizers or educational experts. But, God is using us anyway."

"Another miracle is that God always supplies us with volunteers to complete any task that presents itself. There is no way we could pay for all the help we have received over the years. God has always sent just the right person or group of people with the skills that we required to assist us to do God's work."

If the reader is wondering how much Gene and Lorraine receive in pay for organizing and operating of the Sakila Sponsorship Program, you may be interested to know that they do not take one penny in salary. Everyone working for SSP, including the Andersons, do so as volunteers. No one receives a salary. Even the office expenses are covered by private funds, separate from the SSP income.

At the current time there are 43.6 million people living in Tanzania. 42% of that population is under the age of 14. The median age of the population in Tanzania is 18 years. If the people in Tanzania are to be reached for God, it seems that now is the exact and correct time to do it through Christian education.

The youngsters in Sakila are always asking for "pipi," which is the Swahili word for candy. Well driller Trusty Matheson usually carries a supply of pipi in his pockets to give out to the little children.

One day while in Sakila, two little boys timidly approached Trusty and asked him for pipi. Trusty said that he would give them some but they had to tell him the name of the President of the United States. The kids thought for a while when one of them blurted out, "Sluys-Anderson." Trusty thought for a second and came to a conclusion that the boy's answer was a better response than the correct one. The boys were rewarded with pipi for their answer.

CHAPTER 18:

HAVE COMPASSION, MAKING A DIFFERENCE
(Jude 22)

As a young person, he had been interested in the medical profession and was planning to be a doctor. When Ben Miller enlisted in the United States Navy in 1987, he joined with the stipulation that he would be trained and be allowed to serve as a corpsman. After his active enlistment was completed, Ben desired to further his medical training by enrolling in a pre-medical program at a junior college. While attending classes, Ben received an admission letter from the school's nursing program despite the fact that he was a pre-med student. He thought about that offer for a while and decided to attend the nursing program with a plan to attend medical school later.

While in nursing school, Ben became passionate about the nursing philosophy. Medicine, as Ben discovered, is based on the germ theory which is derived from the fact that medical conditions are caused from disease and diseases have an origin such as a bacteria or germ. If the disease is treated, then the person gets well. Whereas nursing is based on a holistic approach that states, in addition to the medical cure, the human response to disease and healing is unique and specific to each person or family. Helping people manage, adapt, and recover from a disease or injury state is the core of nursing. Even though medicine and nursing have many of the same practices, treating people with the holistic concept appealed to Ben.

Working as a bedside nurse for 10 years, Ben practiced in a busy emergency department, intensive care unit, and post anesthesia care unit until he returned to school to earn a Master's Degree in nursing from Washington State University. With a focus on acute care and family practice, Ben started working as an Advance Practice Registered Nurse (Nurse Practitioner) in a small rural community in north central Idaho providing primary care before relocating to Bremerton, Washington to sub-specialize in cardiovascular diseases.

In January 2007, Ben moved his practice to Montana and specialized in emergency medicine and hospital care. In March of that year, Marion Sluys of the Sakila Sponsorship Program contacted Ben about joining a medical team from Washington state who would be traveling to Sakila in October of that year. The team needed someone with Ben's skills to accompany them. Marion then asked Ben if he had any interest in going. The idea struck a pleasing chord with Ben who volunteered for the trip. He even recruited a few more medical personnel to go with the team.

The first team that Ben traveled with consisted of a dentist, two nurse practitioners, two nurses, two x-ray technicians and group of support people. In total, twelve people traveled from Seattle, Washington to Tanzania for three weeks of volunteer medical work among the Meru tribe who live between Mount Meru and Mount Kilimanjaro.

Ben remembers the first trip to Tanzania as the most challenging experience of his life. This was mainly due to the fact that he had no idea what he was getting into. The medical team was predominately based out of Port Angeles, WA. No member of the group had ever been to Sakila previously with only two members of the team having ever been on a mission trip before. He soon realized that he was 8,000 miles from home. Even though he was in a very lush tropical area, Ben appreciated the fact that he was in a culture that was real and certainly different from what he was used to.

When most westerners go on a safari visit to Tanzanian parks, they are kept in protected islands of western culture where English is spoken and American style food is served in a manner consistent with American or European dining. In contrast, when the medical team arrived in Sakila, they found that they were immersed not only in a Christian community, but also in a tribal lifestyle. Ben learned to say little and keep a low profile to minimize the chances of violating customs of the local culture.

But keeping a low profile does not always work. As noted before, village elders, evangelism school staff, Bishop Eliudi, and western visitors meet every day for coffee at 4 P.M. Since the Meru tribal culture is male dominated, all important men were expected to be at the coffee. Of the medical team that was visiting Sakila, Ben was one of three men in the group. As a result, he was considered as one of the leaders of the team.

Instead of attending the coffee time on his first day in Sakila, Ben was attracted to the church choir practice. The beautiful, dynamic, and hypnotic melodies of a cappella singing had captured his intrigue and curiosity. However, by missing the ritualistic coffee time, he had been discourteous to the school leaders. Later that evening members of the school staff effectively informed Ben that missing the afternoon coffee time was a serious breach of etiquette and was considered an insult. Aware of his serious social blunder, Ben made sure that he never missed coffee time again unless he was traveling away from Sakila.

The process of coffee time starts with a formal greeting to Bishop Eliudi. Next, a greeting processional is conducted to each person in the group with a hand shake and "jambo" (hello). This time is spent in fellowship and enjoyment of coffee with "sugar" or "no sugar". Tanzanian coffee is one of the finest coffees ever tasted and grown on the local farms in the shade of the banana trees. The beans are allowed to slowly mature and contain a silky smooth flavor. Many Tanzanians enjoy a healthy dose of raw sugar in their coffee; sometimes changing the concept to drinking "a little coffee with your sugar".

The process of coffee time is more than fellowship. It is a time for developing friendships and long lasting relationships. As a group of Americans visiting Sakila for the first time, the circle consists of mzungus (white people) sitting on one side and Tanzanians sitting on the other side of the circle. By the end of a visit, guests and locals will be sitting mixed together, with visitors practicing the minute amount of Swahili they have learned. The Tanzanians smile and laugh at the pronunciation, the dialect, or even the unrecognizable vocabulary. Missing the coffee hour was more than a cultural insult; it is missing a wonderful cultural experience of friendship.

As it has been said, "food is fuel." The medical team's concern about having enough to eat in Sakila did not become something to worry about. However, there was an incredible degree of consistency in the Tanzanian diet. A regular staple is ugali, a corn meal loaf which is enjoyed at many meals including breakfast. Many local village meals are based on a bean, corn or rice base with many fresh fruits and vegetables. Being guests, visitors are served the very best the village has to offer. In Sakila many of the lunches and dinners consisted of meat stew (either beef or goat) over a bed of rice. On occasion, the cooks would provide a taste of home with popcorn.

Ben was not prepared for the food that the team was served. It was so un-American in nature and, when properly prepared, healthier than what he normally ate. Meals in Sakila are really a detoxification from a typical American diet. Breakfast was a light meal of an egg and fruit. Lunch and dinner were pretty nearly identical: a boiled meat in a stew served over a layer of rice, pasta or beans. Fresh tropical fruit was constantly available from local trees. All a person had to do was pick it off of the tree, wash it and enjoy.

When travelling to outlying villages for remote clinics, the women of the church would provide morning coffee and lunch for the medical teams. Perceptively, the medical team was provided the "very best" food in the village, which would include chicken, roasted corn, pineapple, watermelon, and oranges. Many of these meals also contain sodas from the local duka (store).

Food storage and preparation are a constant concern with food borne illnesses. Only a very small percentage of village people have electricity and even fewer of those people have refrigeration. Although dysentery is somewhat controlled in Sakila, when the medical team traveled to outlying villages, members feared becoming ill from the food. In those villages, running water is not usually available and hand washing by the inhabitants is very limited. If hand washing was accomplished, there typically was not a lot of soap employed with the water. Whenever a team member began to feel ill, the leader of the medical group started giving antibiotics to that person.

Statistically speaking, a person runs a 10% chance of acquiring a local disease for each week that they are visiting in a country similar to Tanzania. If a person stays three weeks in country, they then have a 30% chance of acquiring a local disease. During a ten week stay, a person has almost a 100% chance of becoming ill.

In addition to the warmer climate, the early mornings, and the consistency of food, there were other ecological challenges. Being in a tropical environment, there are a large number of reptiles and insects which take up residence inside the houses, as well as outside. All of those creatures seem to be much bigger in Africa, and specifically in Tanzania.

In particular, the local insects are huge. There are carpenter bees that are the size of an adult male's thumb and have a stinger that is 1 inch long. These bugs will dig out a nest inside a tree using the stinger and then hide inside the wood.

Cockroaches are the size of Texas cockroaches and have aggressive personalities. At night if you turn on the light, the cockroaches will actually charge at you before retreating. During one of the trips, a jumbo cockroach ran across the foot of one of the members on the team while she was in the washroom. Rather than running, she came prancing out of the bathroom and leaped onto the couch.

The other critters that make themselves at home are the geckos. They are able to crawl through the air vents installed in the building walls and will curl up next to you for a nap.

One female team member had a phobia of the geckos that populate the village. As a result, she took all the necessary steps to prevent the friendly little critters from coming to her bedroom. She put paper over the vents and sealed them with duct tape and kept her windows closed. One night while getting ready for bed, she discovered a gecko stowaway in her room and came out screaming. The rest of the team was sent on a seek, capture, and remove mission (although she would have preferred a seek and destroy mission) to render her sleeping quarters as a "gecko-free zone."

Registered nurse Vanessa Grimsland was manning the Sakila health clinic in October of 2012. She was staying in the guest rooms attached to Bishop Eliudi's home. One very dark night, she was in bed when she was awakened by strange sounds in her bedroom. Since Vanessa always kept her flashlight on the stand by her bed, she reached for it to investigate the sounds. However in the darkness, she could not locate the light. The strange noises grew louder and more frequent. Vanessa knew that going back to sleep was out of the question. But as hard as she tried, she could not find the flashlight.

As she began to panic, she realized that she would have to jump out of bed to reach the overhead light switch that was located on the opposite wall of the room. Steeling her resolve, she threw back the bed covers and leaped from the mattress towards the switch. Luckily she quickly found it and turned on the overhead light. Vanessa swiftly discovered that there were black frogs hopping all about her bare feet. Those frogs ranged in size from two to four inches across their backs. The frogs were everywhere on the floor and clinging to the lower edges of her window curtains and bed blankets. When the light came on, they started hopping into the air in frantic leaps.

Vanessa ran and opened the front door of her apartment and screamed for help. It was then that she saw the entire patio floor outside her door was a sea of black frogs. Those frogs were pouring into her living compartment. (When the door was closed, the frogs had squeezed into her living room through a gap between the door bottom and the threshold.) According to Vanessa, the scene reminded her of one of the Biblical plagues detailed in the book of Exodus. After Eliudi's housekeeper came to her rescue, they spent the rest of the night sweeping the frogs from the rooms. After that experience, Vanessa rolled a towel up and stuffed it under the outside door to keep any more creatures from entering her domain.

When people think of human health conditions in Africa, diseases such as HIV/AIDS, tuberculosis, malaria, dengue fever, and even Ebola come to mind. Before he went to Sakila, Ben expected to see numerous people with infectious diseases such as dengue fever or malaria arriving at the clinic to be treated. He found that chronic diseases do happen at various places around the world, but common medical conditions exist everywhere. Sore throats, back pain, colds or injuries were by far the most encountered conditions treated.

On different days, there were as many as 200 people arriving at the clinic for evaluation. Normally the number of daily patients screened was between 60 and 80. Some of the sick or injured would arrive the night before to be in line the first thing in the morning. The clinic volunteers worked all day with an established time to close the clinic in the evening. If some of those seeking medical help arrived too late in the day to be seen, they sometimes stayed in Sakila for the following day's screenings.

One of the tasks that medical teams accomplished while in Tanzania was to administer anti-parasite medicines to everyone in the area. Intestinal parasites are a big problem in Africa. The failure to eliminate intestinal worms is the leading cause of anemia and mental retardation in children. The prescribed treatment for intestinal parasites is effective for about three months. Hopefully, a new medical team would be arriving in Sakila within that time to start the process all over again.

During Ben's first visit to Sakila, a two week old baby was brought to the clinic that was born two weeks premature. The baby was barely bigger than Ben's hand. Babies are supposed have heart rates of 140 to 160 beats per minute. This boy's heart rate was less than 100. Its body temperature was down to 95 degrees. To Ben these conditions were indicators that the baby was going to die. It was clear to the medical team, the baby needed more care than could be provided at the clinic.

With the help from some of the team members and the use of Bishop Eliudi's Land Rover, the baby and mother were driven to the government hospital in Arusha where the team was told to take the baby home and to "stop trying to breast feed the baby. If you just sit the baby up and have him drink from a cup, he will be fine." Appalled at the advice from the government doctor, the baby was taken to a local private Christian hospital for a second opinion.

There the Medical Officer on duty agreed the baby was ill and needed to be hospitalized, but those services are limited in Tanzania. The nearest hospital with equipment to manage a premature neonate was in Moshi, at the Kilimanjaro Christian Medical Center (KCMC), located 50 kilometers away. The Officer wrote a medical referral for the team member in order to have the baby admitted to KCMC. However by that time, it was dark and unsafe to travel to Moshi. The baby and mother were returned to their home for the night.

The next morning, armed with a referral from the second hospital, some pocket money and a fresh driver, a medical team member was prepared for the journey to Moshi. God was watching over the baby that night; with divine care, the baby had survived. After arriving at the hospital in Moshi, the baby was admitted to the intensive care unit. At a cost of $400, his hospital bill was paid in advance. He remained in the hospital for four weeks before being released.

A year and half later when Ben returned to Tanzania, he checked up on the baby to see how he faired. To Ben's delight, he was alive and healthy as any other toddler in the area.

Before Ben left Montana with the first team, he was under the impression that there was no medical care at all available in Tanzania. From the journey of the pre-mature baby, Ben was enlightened to discover that there were medical services accessible for the general population. Some of the medical care was good and some not so good. Ben found that there were clinics and hospitals, but that they were located in the major urban areas of the country. Consequently, few services were available to residents in the rural settings. Delivering a sick person to an established medical resource was an arduous all day journey in most cases. Many ill or injured Tanzanian people will forgo medical treatment to save themselves the difficulty of traveling the long distances.

Ben and his fellow team members found the old clinic building in Sakila was adequate but very basic. The three room building that had been constructed in 1997 was still in use. It had been sheet rocked to keep the birds and rodents out of the facility. One room in the clinic was set aside for interviewing patients. Another room that served as a pharmacy had rows of shelves in it. Available supplies and medications were organized there. The screening room was equipped with chairs and tables that were used by the team for patient medical examinations.

In order to compensate for the conditions they encountered, at times the team had to modify their standard Western procedures. Sometimes the overhead lights worked and sometimes they did not. The electrical power to the clinic was dependent on the electricity supplied by the Tanzanian public utilities. When electricity was not available, the team used flashlights or wore headlamps during their examinations.

The doctors that traveled with the medical teams to Sakila performed just a limited amount of surgical operations on the patients. With the way the first clinic is constructed, mold and fungus were hard to control. There really was no way to establish a sterile environment at the old clinic to perform surgical operations other than very minor procedures.

Before performing an operation, the medical staff has to ask the question, "And then what?" That question reminds the doctor who may open a body that they have to ask themselves what will happen after the operation is completed. What will be the chances of the patient becoming infected as a result of the operation? (Any time that the skin is cut for surgery, the risk of infection increases.) What is the chance of the patient having a normal life after the operation? Will we make them better or will we make them worse? Is the treatment better or worse than not performing it? This thought process is called risk stratification. Usually if a patient has severe pain or disfiguration, or the problem is life threating, the doctors do what they can to alleviate the situation by surgery. If a patient arrives with a non-life threating condition such as a lymphoma (a benign fatty growth) where it cannot be seen by other people, an operation is not performed at the clinic.

There were times at the clinic when a patient arrived for treatment that simply could not be helped. As a result of the medical screening, the staff would become aware that the person's condition was terminal. All that the medical staff could do for those patients was lay their hands on them and pray for them. As Ben says, "Life and death walk hand-in-hand in Africa. Sometimes you have to step over the dying to save the one who can be healed."

Ben's team also provides "well child care" for the orphans at Christ Hope Orphanage near the IEC church in Arusha. Each orphan has an individual medical chart which is updated during the yearly visits. The medical team checks the children's height and weight; examines the children for anemia, or any other substandard condition. Ben reports that the orphaned children are in good physical condition and are well taken care of. As the medical providers examine the children, the support staff plays soccer with the kids or puts on puppet shows for the youngsters.

CHAPTER 19:

HEAL EVERY DISEASE AND SICKNESS

(Matthew 10:1)

Medical teams that Ben Miller has been a part of have based most of their work in Sakila. However, two or three excursions during each visit are made to outlying villages. Into the bed of a truck, the team would load what supplies they would be using or thought that they might need during the day. These outings may take them a few kilometers or up to thirty kilometers from Sakila. The village picked for the one day clinics are selected by Bishop Eliudi from information and requests received from his network of IEC pastors.

On arriving in a distant village, the medical team sets up in an IEC church building to conduct the remote clinic. The team then screens everyone that comes to them for help. The team tries to remain there until everyone wanting help is at least examined. Sometimes this practice causes the team to arrive back in Sakila late at night. Occasionally more than 150 people are examined on a typical day in the outlying villages.

During one trip to Tanzania, Ben's medical team traveled to a village that had never been visited by a medical doctor. There the team saw the most horrific cases of malnutrition, abuse, and chronic disease. Katie Culbertson is a dietitian who had traveled to Sakila before. That year her participation on the team was critical as there were two serious cases of malnutrition resulting in advance stages of rickets and starvation. Her training and understanding of nutritional requirements were essential to developing a plan to provide these families with an ongoing source of food and nutrition.

While the team was in that village, a very thin mother brought her eight year old daughter to be examined by the clinic team. The girl was suffering from rickets, a skeletal bone disease that is caused from malnutrition and the lack of vitamin D. The girl was so ravished from rickets that she had become bow legged, her head was constantly cocked to one side and her spine had started to visibly deform. Basically, all of the girl's bones had started to compress and fail just from her minimal body weight. The girl was losing the ability of her skeleton to support her body. Since her bones and joints could never be returned to normal, the girl's condition was not treatable. Katie and the other members of the team realized that the girl would probably never live to adulthood and were deeply sadden at not being able to remedy the young girl's condition.

After arriving back in Sakila, Katie went to Bishop Eliudi and told him about the mother and daughter that were dying of malnutrition. Katie bought a 200 pound bag of beans from the IEC store in Sakila to deliver it to the mother. Next Katie borrowed a driver and Eliudi's Land Rover to convey the beans to the family. When she returned to the village, she found the family in a hut. To Katie's dismay she discovered that the mother not only had the eight year old daughter, but that she also had seven other children in the mud and stick hovel who were younger than the daughter with rickets.

The family had been surviving on corn as the only staple which is an incomplete protein by itself. With the addition of the beans, the family was provided a complete protein diet. Later the team set up a fund with Godwin and Eliudi that would assure that someone would deliver a bean "care package" to the family once a month year round.

The people of Tanzania have seen the benefits of western medical practices and usually freely allow themselves to be examined and treated. What also encourages the good will of the people towards western medical teams is that the medical care provided is free to all who come seeking help. However there are a number of places in northeast Tanzania that still cling to the witchdoctors and their rituals. Once the people see western medical practices succeed, they quickly abandon the shamans with their illogical ceremonies.

As an example of the witchdoctor's formalities, one traditional remedy for curing malaria has been to mix marijuana with elephant dung. The patient is placed in an enclosed hut where the laced dung is burnt. While the patient inhauls the smoke, the witchdoctor urinates on the malaria patient. After a little thought by the patient and after seeing western medicine succeed, it is hard for Tanzanians to understand how being peed-on will help them.

Since that first trip, Ben has been back to Tanzania four more times. He has become a leader or co-leader on those returning trips. He desires that his teams be half medical workers and half support people. Support workers are non-medical individuals who assist in checking in patients, counting out pills, preparing and cleaning patient areas, etc. To go with a medical team, a person does not need any specialized medical training. They just have to have the desire to help wherever they are needed.

Ben tries to take two or three providers (doctors, nurse practitioners, or physician assistants) in the team with four or five registered nurses or paramedical workers. Nursing students are always a plus to have in the team as the students are a great help and they receive some very practical experience. Pharmacists, occupational therapists, physical therapists, massage therapists, dietitians, and dentists also are among some of the trained medical staff that can be included in the teams. Sometimes it is not really clear what those medical professions are going to accomplish while they are in Africa, but there is always something for them to do to assist others if their specialty is not in demand at the moment.

Judy Kinley at the IEO office in Poulsbo, WA currently schedules the medical teams so that there is just one group at a time visiting Sakila. Despite these scheduling practices, the medical ministry is really working to God's plan. During the summer of 2012, two groups were inadvertently scheduled to visit Sakila at the same time. Ben's group was from Montana, while the other team was from Maryland. An impromptu plan was agreed upon for each medical team to practice independently and at different locations. Because of circumstances and a family illness, the only doctor and leader on the Maryland team had to withdraw. Because both teams were there at the same time, they merged into one large medical team. Ben was able to step in and lead both teams by providing guidance and support for the Maryland group. Many members of Team Maryland had never been on a medical mission trip and even fewer had ever been to Sakila before. The sleeping arrangements became a bit complicated and crowded with almost 30 visitors in Sakila, but God worked it to the advantage of all concerned.

Health care is different in Tanzania than it is in the United States. As an example, Ben took a woman who was about to deliver a baby to the public hospital in Arusha. Since he thought that there might be complications during the delivery, Ben checked her in. The admissions clerk said that the lady would probably be in the hospital for fourteen days and wanted to know who was going to pay her bill. Ben agreed to pay the lady's fee and asked how much was the charge was going to be. He was told that for the two week stay for maternity and post-partum care, the hospital charged a dollar a day. He gladly paid the $14. (The bill for major surgery at a public hospital in Tanzania is generally no more than $300 to $400.)

Ben and his medical team were preparing to travel back to Sakila in early 2011. The team relies on monetary and material donations to stock their medical and generic supplies. During the packing of those supplies, a person in Montana gave the team two boxes of baby formula. Since most women in Tanzania breast feed their infants, Ben felt that maybe they did not need to take the formula along with them. Besides the doubtful need of the formula, the two boxes weighed a considerable amount. Usually all of the medical supplies are trucked to Poulsbo, WA from Montana to be loaded into a container that will be shipped later to Tanzania. At those times, the weight of the items shipped is not a concern. However in 2011, the team was scheduled to arrive in May before the containers were supposed to be delivered to Sakila. That year the team would have to transport all of their donated supplies in their checked-in luggage at the airport. Weight was a major concern. Ben believed that taking the formula along would cost more to ship than it was worth and twice ordered it left in America.

When the team set up shop in Sakila in May 2011, Baby Claire was brought to the clinic. A mother who was nursing her two week old baby had recently witnessed her mother being murdered. This traumatic event caused the woman's breast milk to permanently cease. To remedy the situation, the mother tried to feed the baby cow's milk diluted with water. When the child came to the clinic, she was starving. The baby was very small and had no baby fat left on her body and was close to death. The mother pleaded for help for Baby Claire. However, the team needed infant formula quickly if they were to save the baby.

One of the members of the team was watching the diagnoses of Baby Claire and saw the hopelessness on the faces of the staff and plainly stated, "Why don't we use the formula that we brought along?" It seems that even though Ben had requested that the cases of formula be left in America, someone had packed them anyway. Without having to pay extra airline fees, the formula had arrived in Sakila with the team. Without further delay, Baby Claire was started on the life-saving formula. That procedure bought the team a week and half period to nurse the baby back to health. During that interval a lactating goat was found and bought to provide milk for Claire after the formula ran out. (Goat milk has been found to be superior in nutrients to cow's milk for feeding new-born babies.)

When the team returned to Sakila in 2012, Baby Claire and her mother re-visited to the clinic. The baby was alive, growing and beautiful. Ben Miller says to this day that he is humbled by the way God provides for His people.

At this time, the new clinic is still being built. Its construction was started in 2009. The new clinic would need an infusion of $50,000 to finish the construction of the building. Then some supplies and medical treatment furnishings will have to be purchased. However, a lot of the equipment required to furnish the new clinic is already in hand. As stated before, there will be an area in the clinic for two operating rooms. There is also a medical lab being planned to provide basic laboratory testing and x-rays. The most important part of the clinic will be providing a community classroom to provide health education.

Ben estimates that just $100,000 can complete the furnishings of the clinic. One of the items that Ben really wants to acquire for the clinic is a digital x-ray machine. That machine generates x-rays in the usual manner, except for the fact that it produces a digitized image. The advantage of a digitized x-ray machine is that it instantly shows the results of the x-ray on a computer screen. There is no waiting for the film to be developed or the storage of chemicals to develop the film, chemicals that can expire. If the medical staff runs across something that they are not familiar with, they can email the x-ray to any doctor in the world who is willing to help them diagnose the situation. Correct and effective treatments can be started on the patient within a very short length of time. A used digital x-ray machine costs about $40,000 in the United States.

Of course, computers will also be mandatory in the new clinic to keep records. Some paper records at the current clinic have been devoured by insects. Solar panels will need to be installed on the roof of the new clinic to provide an inexpensive source of energy for the computers and medical equipment. With the panels and an operational generator, a constant supply of power can be assured when used in conjunction with the sporadic public electricity source.

There are specialized doctors from various locations in the United States that are ready to travel to Tanzania to work at the new Sakila clinic. Some of the human physical conditions that can be remedied at the new clinic will be cleft palates, hernias and eye cataracts. The main thing that the doctors who perform such operations require is a satisfactory working environment. The new clinic will provide that work area.

After the clinic is completed, Bishop Eliudi hopes to have a full time medical staff at the facility. It is hoped that Tanzanian doctors and nurses will someday staff the clinic to lessen the dependency on western medical personnel. Tanzanian medical personnel will also better understand the language and customs of the people that they treat. They will know how to best draw out required medical information from the patients. Detailed histories of the patients will become easier to maintain.

After five trips to Sakila, Ben Miller has a good working relationship with Bishop Eliudi and spends as much time with Eliudi as he can. Ben considers Bishop Eliudi to be a true friend. Eliudi has so many projects going on at one time that he is like a miraculous juggler trying to keep all his projects functioning at once. Ben also feels that one of Eliudi's top personal attributes is his ability to develop personal relationships with just about everyone he meets.

In 2012 Ben was in Sakila and completing his PhD degree in nursing at Washington State University. His PhD dissertation was the study of diabetes in rural Tanzania. Before doing some medical investigating in Tanzania, Ben was required to fly to Dar es Salaam to get his research approved by the Tanzanian government. Eliudi decided to assist Ben in Dar es Salaam and traveled with him. While they were there, Ben mentioned that he really wanted to see the Indian Ocean.

Eliudi found a cab driver and convinced the driver to go off of the meter to drive them around Dar es Salaam for the entire day. The cab driver then took them everywhere they wanted to go. When Ben and Eliudi had a meeting with government officials during the day, they left their personal belongings in the cab under the watchful eye of the driver. The cab and the belongings were still secure when they come back from the meetings.

Finally towards the end of the day, the cab arrived at the shore of the Indian Ocean. After parking, Eliudi and Ben walked down to the water to do a bit of site seeing. When they arrived back at the cab, there was a group of men sitting under a palm tree near the car. One member of the group blocked Ben and Eliudi's access to the cab and demanded money for protecting the cab while they were walking on the beach. It was clear to Ben that the man was serious about robbing them, if not doing them serious bodily harm.

It is at that point that Eliudi's ability to develop one-to-one relationships took over the situation. To the thug, Eliudi calmly explained, "Friend, we did not hire you to watch our cab. The driver is satisfactorily doing that." The man sneered and said that he and his friends saw to it that the driver was not robbed or that the cab was not damaged by having its windows broken out. The man was really hostile and angry and wanted all the money that Eliudi and Ben had.

At that point Eliudi started to turn on the charm by joking and laughing with the would-be robber. Even though Ben could not understand the words spoken in Swahili, the demeanor of the thug seemed to soften as Bishop Eliudi chatted with him. In a short while Eliudi took a small bill out of his pocket and pressed it into the man's hand. When Eliudi left the thug, the man seemed to feel that Eliudi was one of the nicest men that he had ever met and that somehow he was not as rich as he thought that he should have been at that point. Ben and Eliudi climbed back into the cab before a very nervous cab driver delivered them back to the airport.

It was Eliudi's ability to work with people that saved the day on the Indian Ocean beach. It was also that ability combined with God's help that keeps the International Evangelism Church thriving in Africa.

CHAPTER 20:
STAND FIRM TO THE END
(Matthew 10:22)

Previously the farthest I had traveled on a mission trip was 200 miles. That was a road trip to the west side of Chicago from near my childhood home in Iowa. That certainly was not a long trip, but it got my mind thinking about missions and helping people in need.

In October 2012 I found myself on an airplane descending to my final destination at the Kilimanjaro Airport. I was about 9,000 air miles into my trip at that point and looking forward to getting off of the airplane. I knew that the Kilimanjaro Airport would be paved to safely land the Boeing 777 in which I was flying. However, I had read that Tanzania has 124 airports and only 9 were paved.

I mentally checked off what I had read about Tanzania. Tanzania was one of the world's poorest countries in terms of per-capita income. I was told that the average yearly income for people living near Sakila was about $150 per year. Agriculture is 25% of the nation's economy with 80% of the nation's workforce employed in that endeavor. Agricultural products comprise 85% of the country's exports. Some of the country's leading exports are coffee, sisal (twine), tea and cashews. Tourism is one of the nation's biggest revenue generators as foreigners flock to Tanzania to see its wildlife or to climb Mt. Kilimanjaro. That mountain's top reaches 19,340 feet in elevation and is the highest point on the African continent. Of the religious people in Tanzania, 35% of them are Muslim, 35% hold indigenous tribal beliefs and 30% are Christian.

I was traveling to Tanzania to interview Bishop Eliudi Issangya and the people close to him, those who knew him the best. I had met Bishop Eliudi many times before when he was touring the United States and visiting his supporting churches and individuals. Now I was going to conduct interviews with him for this biography in his native land. I also wanted to see Sakila and its environs. Having heard of the work that Eliudi was accomplishing in Africa, I would soon witness it first-hand. I had come to find out why some people have called Eliudi Issangya the "Billy Graham of Tanzania."

What had always impressed me about Eliudi's mission was that he had no large American or European church denomination financially supporting him. Bishop Eliudi made his ministry work from a totally volunteer group of mostly community churches in North America. God opened opportunities for Eliudi in those churches and he nurtured those contacts. Of course, without an overseas religious denomination overseeing his work, Eliudi was left to develop his African ministry as he believed God was leading him. In my next few weeks I would see this miracle that God had brought about in Africa through his loyal servant, Eliudi Issangya.

There is no doubt that Bishop Eliudi has made lasting impressions on the people he meets and has had major impact on their lives both in North America and in Africa. The following is a story of a young American girl who met Eliudi. It was told to me by her grandfather, Dick Lunt.

Terry and Kim Trent are the parents of Katelynn Trent. Terry and Kim became associates of Bishop Eliudi when they were living in Jamul, California. Bishop Eliudi had often come to their church to itinerate and raise money for his ministry. During those times, Terry, Kim and Bishop Eliudi became very good friends. When he was in Jamul, they would spend a lot of time discussing and praying for the ministry in Tanzania.

Because of their relationship with Bishop Eliudi, their daughter, Katelynn, got to know and respect him while he was in Jamul. She would follow him around like a puppy dog, absorbing everything she could glean from him. What an awesome thing it was to see such a busy man of God willing to spend time with a young person, investing in her future. That sounds just like something Jesus would do. One day, when she was about 8 and 1/2 years old, Eliudi and Katelynn had a very in-depth conversation, which went on for several hours, regarding the Christian mission field in Africa. That dialogue made a very deep, life changing, impression on Katelynn.

About 6 months later, she was alone in her bedroom praying and seeking the Lord for direction for her life. She emerged from her bedroom, asking her mother and father to talk with her.

While talking with them she told them that, she had been diligently and reverently praying when God very clearly spoke to her about her future. She told them that she did not know where or when but she was convinced that God had told her, that sometime in the future, she would become a Christian missionary and that she would serve the Lord in a foreign land. God would lead and prepare her to show her the way. His word told her that "He would be a lamp unto her feet and a light unto her path" to guide her through the process.

Since that time Katelynn began an insatiable quest to get to know the Lord in an even deeper and personal way. In an effort to speed up the learning process, she became enrolled in both home high school and a junior college. Katelynn was soon awarded a certificate to teach English as a second language.

During her high school years she went on five short-term mission trips with Calvary Chapel of Fort Lauderdale, FL. During her last short-term trip to a fully Muslim country in North Africa, she fell absolutely in love with the people, the country and with the possibility of serving God there. She spoke to and prayed with her parents about her vision. After a lot of prayer, counseling and much preparation, she was then in a position to go to the mission field at the ripe old age of 19 years. After all of the usual painful hoops were jumped through, she was on her way for her first one-year commitment of being a missionary in Northern Africa.

Since then she has completed an additional one year term and is now half way through another two year commitment. In Africa, she is a teacher of English to mainly teenaged children plus a few adults. Through her own study she is becoming fluent in the Arabic language.

Recently Katelynn was asked what she thought her role in life was. Her response was, "I believe my responsibility is to lay down my life. Not necessarily in death, although it may come to that, but in everything. I want to live so that people around me say, 'That is why I will became a Christian. Christ is real in you. You walk a straight path and your words follow your actions.'" This commitment of Katelynn's for people in Africa was nurtured years before when she had her talk with a busy man named Eliudi, who took the time to talk with an inquisitive youngster.

That is just one example of a person's life being changed after meeting Bishop Eliudi. (I want to thank Dick Lunt for letting me use this story.)

Of course, the biggest impact by Eliudi in people's lives has been in Africa. The story of Sophia and her mother, Juliana, comes to mind. Sophia was the youngest of three children of Juliana and her husband. One day the husband divorced Juliana, took the two older male children and left Sophia and her mother without any means of support. Juliana found making a living extremely difficult after that. They did not have a place to live until a local man allowed them to sleep in his goat shed where he stored goat food and housed his goats. Sophia and her mother lived with the goats in those filthy conditions for three years.

While the pair was living in the goat shed, Juliana would go out every day looking for any work that she could get paid for. One day while her mother was away, a group of men severely molested Sophia. That crime left Sophia with physical and mental scars related to the molestation. Her mother was traumatized by the event to a point where she could not leave Sophia alone or venture forth to look for work. It was soon thereafter that some people from Eliudi's school found Sophia and Juliana in the goat shed.

Juliana and Sophia were brought to the IEC campus for shelter. Eventually Juliana was offered a job as gardener at the Sluys-Anderson Primary School, which Juliana accepted. Along with the pay for the job, a house was found by the primary school staff where she and Sophia could live. The rent for the house was $10 per month. Sophia was then enrolled at the primary school and is receiving an education there. In response to all of this goodwill, Juliana said, "Now I know that God can see me."

Juliana continues to struggle, but at least she has hope with Jesus in her heart. Bishop Eliudi may not have had a direct intervention in Juliana and Sophia's life, but through his teaching and example, others are following Jesus's kindness for his people.

Nor was the Christian kindness lost on Juliana. When she was able to steadily work as the primary school gardener, Juliana searched and found two homeless children who were just a few years younger than Sophia.

When she located those kids, she took them into her home to care for and feed them. When you take kids into your home in Tanzania, there is no compensation coming from the government. The person who houses the children is solely responsible for their support.

When I was able to conduct my interviews, I repeatedly asked one question of the people who knew Bishop Eliudi Issangya the best. What did they see as Eliudi's strongest character point? To that I received numerous responses. John Mathew said that he believed that Eliudi's stoutest trait was that he was a strong leader. John believed that Eliudi knew where God was leading him and the School of Evangelism, and he was going to take everyone along who wanted to go with him. Moses Mafie said that he thought the answer to the question was that Bishop Eliudi just simply loves to do God's work.

When I asked Eliudi's daughter, Rogathe, the same question, she had a different response. Even though it seemed to some that Eliudi had neglected his family at times, Rogathe's answer was that her father really loves people. In fact she said that Eliudi loves people more than he loves himself. Eliudi sees the bigger need that others do not see and does what seems to be impossible to fulfill that need. Rogathe now knows that Eliudi loves his family very much. And she is proud of what he has accomplished to better Africa, even though she and her siblings had to do without some material needs for a period of time.

His wife, Lucy, had yet another answer. She has not been with Eliudi since the beginning of his ministry as the others have. As a result, Lucy has a little different perspective. She said that Eliudi is a bishop and head of nearly 2,000 established churches in Central Africa. Even so, he is still a down-to-earth man. Some people get so heavenly minded that they are no earthly good. It is only an eighth of a mile from Eliudi's office to his home over what some have called the Avocado Lane. It may take Eliudi an hour to travel that quarter mile, because, if someone wants to converse with him, the Bishop stops and talks with them. That person could be John Mathew, his number two man, or a new student at the School of Evangelism who wants a moment of Eliudi's time. Whoever that person is, he or she will get Eliudi's attention as he listens to whatever is on that individual's mind.

Even young children are deserving of his time.

Eliudi may be the head of the International Evangelism Church and has a nice big office on the second floor of the IEC headquarters building; but he prefers the old office in the one story building that was first built on the one acre his father gave him. He is closer to the school and the students from that office. There he is closer to the land and the mission that God has given him.

POST SCRIPT #1:

Bishop Eliudi Issangya gave the following speech to supporters of his Tanzania ministries in Poulsbo, WA on 28 Jan 2012. This address was presented at the annual Sakila Sponsorship dinner that informed the sponsors of the students at the Sluys/Anderson Primary School and the Sakila Hebron Secondary School of current issues and progress.

To speak about the ministry going on in Africa, [I have to say] God is so good. All the time we are experiencing miracles. When we say miracles, we mean that what men cannot do; we let God do what men cannot do. We are so excited to know that God is good to us and he has anointed us; not just me, not just volunteer leaders, but has anointed all of us as the body of Christ. God has called us to fulfill His purpose. So look back to 2003 when we started the vision of the primary school and then look at the miracle of where we are today. You have 700 kids getting an education at the primary school. You have the high school built and classes started there. God acquired the land and buildings for the schools. That is done.

That is a good place to say "Amen" and give God a great hand!

In 1983 I came to Bainbridge Island and met Bob and Adele Smith. I met them at their church and shared the vision [of a Bible School]. It is a wonderful thing to see how far we have come since then and the accomplishments that we can testify of and rejoice in. It is all because God has walked with us. And it is a good thing to say that you are walking with God.

One morning Moses was in the desert and going to the Promised Land. Moses said to God, "Help us because we cannot go without you. We want to walk with you all the way." In 1983, I came to this area and met many friends. Today we have so many more friends supporting the ministry. God has walked with us from the beginning - from the Bible School to where we are today.

But here is what I want to tell you this evening. Jacob went to Laban to find himself a wife. He saw the woman he wanted to marry. He worked for her for seven years. But when the time was up after the seven years, Jacob was cheated. He was given another wife that he really did not want. Jacob went to Laban and complained that Laban did not give him what he wanted. But, Jacob would work for another seven years for the woman he loved. So he worked 14 years for his chosen wife.

Sometimes I wonder if we love Jesus as Jacob loved his wife. My friends, God loved us so much that he died on the cross because He loved us so much. The question is do we love God as much as He loves us? God loves us so much. We have to love him as much as Jacob loved his wife that he was willing to work the extra years.

Today, God is asking for our heart. How much are we willing to give to Him? So my friends, I appreciate how much you have done since 2003 and how much you have accomplished. Because you loved God so much, you want to go extra. You are not going to say that it is all over now. You are ready to go the extra mile for God.

You have taken and educated the primary kids for seven years. Now it is time to educate those same kids for four more years through High School in order to get the pilots, teachers, presidents, doctors and ministers the world desperately needs. You have accomplished something. However if we quit now, we will have no doctors. If we quit now, we will have no teachers. If we quit now, we will have no pilots. If we quit now, we will have no ministers. We still have to go the extra mile. We have started the work, but we still have to keep working to get those doctors out.

That is a good place to shout "Amen!"

When you retire and come to visit us in Sakila, your child that you sponsored will meet you and take you by airplane as your pilot to where you want to go. So when you come to Tanzania, your child will be there to meet you at the airport. But the work is not done and you have not yet retired. We have work to do and God is going to bless that work so that it bears fruit.

I still have a few words to say to you from 1 Corinthians 15:58. "Therefore my dear brothers, stand firm. Let nothing move you. Always give yourselves fully to the work of the Lord, because you know that your labor in the Lord is not in vain." So stand fast and let nothing move you. Always give yourselves fully to the Lord, we are not done yet. Do not go halfway. Go fully until you get the pilots. Until you get the doctors. This is your testimony – I have accomplished what God wanted me to do to get the doctors and teachers. Your school will change a country!

And you know that the labor that you do in the Lord is not in vain. It is not for our pride. What we do for children, we do for the Lord. When we help a child, we help the Lord. Your work is not in vain as it has been a blessing for you and your child. So my friends give yourselves fully to God, not half way. Give yourself fully to God until you finish the job. Give until the Lord says, "Thank you my daughter! Thank you my son! You have done what I sent you to do." Praise the Lord!

From Matthew 10, "Whoever finds his life will lose it, and whoever loses his life for my sake will find it. He who receives you receives me, and he who receives me receives the one who sent me. Anyone who receives a prophet because he is a prophet will receive a prophet's reward, and anyone who receives a righteous man will receive a righteous man's reward." Now listen to the next part very carefully. "And if anyone gives even a cup of cold water to one of these little ones because he is my disciple, I tell you the truth, he will certainly not lose his reward." God never lies. I tell you the truth, this is Jesus speaking. They are not men's words. It is Jesus' words. I tell you the truth; you will certainly not lose your reward.

That is a good place to shout "Amen"!

If it was not for Jesus, no one here would know about Sakila. Or know about the Sluys/Anderson Primary School if it were not for Jesus. Because of Jesus, God has opened the door and you know the children of Sakila. God has given you a child or children [to sponsor]. And that is because of Jesus. And because of that you will never, ever lose your reward. That is the word from Jesus! This you know and now remind each other. This is your reward if you help one child.

Every day we give food to the students while they are at school. These are real people who eat real food. It is hard to keep the food supplied. But, it is because of Jesus that we can feed those kids. We have more than 800 students attending our schools. I believe that Jesus is looking down at us from Heaven and saying, "Well done my faithful children! Keep doing it!" Many families are rejoicing because of you. My friends, I want to encourage you. You are doing a good job. And one day you will be truly blessed. Not just when you go to heaven, but when you retire and go to Tanzania to see what the children are doing. And they will thank you for the rice. They were only five years old then. When they grow up and you retire from your labors, they will thank you. When they graduate, those kids will know that they are to do something [with their lives]. They will thank you for their education and their good homes because of what you have given them. So when you come to Tanzania, how glad you will be. So do not get tired or lose your heart. Do not give up as your work is not completed. Continue to pray for God's work.

POST SCRIPT #2:

Whenever Bishop Eliudi conducts any sort of meeting in America, he usually has the group in attendance sing with him his favorite song, *Fire, Fire, Fire!* Below are the words to that song in Swahili and English. Eliudi leads the song in both languages.

Fire, Fire, Fire;

Fire fall on me,

    (Repeat)

As in the Day of Pentecost,

Fire fall on me.

    (Repeat)

Moto, Moto, Moto;

Moto Umewaka.

    (Repeat)

Kama Siku Ya Pentecost,

Moto Umewaka.

    (Repeat)

Spirit, Spirit, Spirit;

Spirit fall on me,

As in the Day of Pentecost,

Spirit fall on me.

Roho, Roho, Roho;

Roho Ameshuka,

Kama Siku Ya Pentecost,

Roho Ameshuka.

Power, Power, Power;

Power fall on me,

As in the Day of Pentecost,

Power fall on me.

Nguvu, Nguvu, Nguvu;

Nguvu Zimeshuka,

Kama Siku Ya Pentecost,

Nguvu Zimeshuka.

POST SCRIPT #3:

English:	Swahili:
Hello	Jambo
Goodbye	Kwa heri
Please	Tafadhali
Welcome	Karibu
Yes, No	Ndiyo, Hapana
My name is …	Jina langu ni …
What is your name?	Jina lako nani?
I am glad to meet you	Ninafurahi kukuona
How are you?	Habari gani?
Fine, Thanks.	Mzuri, Asante.
Not very well	Si wazima sana wanaumwa.
Lady	Akinamama
Gentleman	Akinababa
What time is it?	Ni saa ngapi?
One, Two, Three	Moja, Mbili, Tatu
Four, Five, Six	Nne, Tano, Sita
Seven, Eight	Saba, Nane
Nine, Ten	Tisa, Kumi
Eleven	Kumi na moja
Twenty-one	Ishirini na moja
Hundred and one	Mia na moja

I am from the United States	Natoka Amerika
I do not understand.	Sifahamu
I understand	Nafahamu
Look out	Angalia
Travel	Safari
Where is …?	… ni wapi?
Men's restroom	Choo cha wanaume
Women's restroom	Choo cha wanawake
Church, School	Kanisa, Shule
Store, Post Office	Duka, Posta
Market	Soko
I am lost	Nimepotea
Straight ahead	Moja kwa moja
Left, Right	Kushoto, Kulia
Forward, Back	Mbele, Nyuma
Danger	Hatari
Slow	Polepole
Stop	Simama
Mosquito net	Chandulua
Soap, Towel	Sabuni, Taulo
I am hungry. (thirsty)	Naona njaa (kiu)
Bread, Sugar	Mkate, Sukari
Salt, Pepper	Chumvi, Pilipili

Beans, Corn	Maharagwe, Mahindi
Rice, Peanuts	Mpunga, Karanga
Eggs, Chicken	Mayai, Kuku
Tea, Coffee	Chai, Kahawa
Candy, Water	Pipi, Maji
Pants, Dress	Suruali, Gauni
Shorts, Skirt	Kaputula, Marinda
Black, Blue, White	Nyeusi, Buluu, Nyeupe
The rainy season	Masika
The dry season	Kiangazi
Sunday, Monday	Jumapipi, Jumatatu
Tuesday, Wednesday	Jumanne, Jumatano
Thursday, Friday	Alhamisis, Ijumaa
Saturday	Jumamosi
It is cold (hot)	Ni baridi (jua kali)
I was bitten by …	Niliumwa na …
Bird, Crocodile	Ndege, Mamba
Cat, Cow	Paka, Ng'ombe
Dog, Donkey	Mbwa, Punda
Elephant, Goat	Tembo, Mbuzi
Giraffe, Hippo	Twiga, Kiboko
Lion, Rhino	Simba, Kifaru
Mosquito, Spider	Mbu, Buibui

Snake, Zebra	Nyoka, Punda milia
Head, Stomach	Kichwa, Tumbo
Arm, Leg	Mkono, Mguu
Hand, Foot	Mkono, Mguu
Eye, Ear, Nose, Mouth	Jicho, Sikio, Pua, Mdomo
Skin, Chest	Ngozi, Kifua
Friend	Rafiki
Child, Children	Mtoto, Watoto
Grandmother	Bibi
Grandfather	Babu
No worries	Hakuna Matana
Praise the Lord	Bwana Asifiwe
Glory to God	Utukufu Kwa Mungo
God bless you	Mungo Akubanki
God is good	Mungo ni Mzun
All the time	Wakati wote
Jesus never fails	Yesu Hakosi
Jesus saves	Yesu Anaokoa
Thank you, Lord	Asante Bwana

POST SCRIPT #4:
Contact Information
International Evangelism Outreach
(IEO)

School of Evangelism

501(c)(3) corporation

Garven Kinley

IEO Office

P.O. Box 1767

Poulsbo, WA 98370

(360) 620-1223

garven@comcast.net

Jan George

(503) 769-5495

mamajan43@yahoo.com

New Hope International Hospital (NHIH) and Clinic

501(c)(3) corporation

Mary Nielsen

(406) 531-7816

mary.nielsen@mso.umt.edu

Christ Hope Orphanage (CHO) &

Crower Trade School

Under IEO 501(c)(3) Corporation

Garven Kinley

IEO Office

P.O. Box 1767

Poulsbo, WA 98370

(360) 620-1223

garven@comcast.net

Jan George

(503) 769-5495

mamajan43@yahoo.com

Sakila Sponsorship Program (SSP)

(Primary, Secondary and High School)

501(c)(3) corporation

PO Box 1430

Poulsbo, WA 98370

www.sakilasponsorship.org

Well Drilling Projects

501(c)(3) corporation

Family Life Church

P.O. Box 214

Gillette, WY 82716

(307) 686-2467

www.ingramcontent.com/pod-product-compliance
Lightning Source LLC
Chambersburg PA
CBHW012106090526
44592CB00019B/2668